THE
LASCAUX PRIZE
VOL 6

THE
LASCAUX PRIZE
VOL 6

edited by
Stephen Parrish
Wendy Russ

ISBN: 978-0-9851666-9-4

Cover design by Wendy Russ.
Cover art by Ivan Aivazovsky, "Ship in the Stormy Sea," oil on canvas, 1887.

Lascaux Books
www.lascauxbooks.com

Contents

continued next page

Poetry Finalists (continued)

Short Story Winner

Short Story Finalists

Editor's Choice Award

Introduction

*T*he *Lascaux Prize Vol 6* is the last to be published as a prize anthology. Beginning next year this publication will serve as an annual print version of *The Lascaux Review*. It will take on a new appearance, but the only difference to the content will be the addition of stories, poems, and essays that also appear online.

Over the years we've published 73 short stories, 47 flash stories, 93 poems, and eight CNF pieces—as editor's choice awards—in these prize anthologies. Fifteen of the contest finalists, thus far, have been the first-ever publications for their authors. Following our inaugural creative nonfiction contest in 2019, *Vol 7* will admit CNF as regular citizens of the Lascaux print community.

Reading contest submissions takes place behind the scenes and is largely a thankless task. We'd like to thank Marguerite Alley, Marissa Glover, Camille Griep, Angela Kubinec, and Shannon Morley-Ragland for putting in the hours. Our mission remains unchanged: to discover quality writing, to acknowledge it, to bring it to light.

Stephen Parrish
Wendy Russ

Aim

by Rebecca Foust

If Pastor Dale's deer-stand was built as a place from which to squeeze a hair trigger, it also ladled up a grand view of the valley below, thick with hickory, sycamore, and elm. Pastor was a righteous man. He called the Sheriff about the untagged does in his neighbor's back shed after finding the guts "bleeding all over the fool's own overdrawn bank statements" in the gulley between their two lots. That's when it began: the curtain-twitch when he passed Ray's house, the footsteps squeaking on snow in the night outside the windows of the doublewide Pastor Dale lived in with his grandson while his daughter got things sorted out in Claysburg.

Pastor Dale was a hunter himself, but always with a license and under his quota. He taught the boy how to track so their quarry would not startle and bolt, tainting the meat, and that a botched shot was worse than coming home empty-handed. In the off-season he dragged a salt lick to the back yard and set out galvanized tins filled with sweet mash and dried corn and kept tallies of the deer and turkeys that came to feed.

The boy wasn't much more interested in hunting then he was in playing ball, where he was like a calf let loose on the field, all folding long legs and more often than not facing away from the play. He daydreamed, read, wanted piano lessons. Everyone knew he couldn't so much as swat a bee. He went along, yes, but used every Sunday School prayer to ask for bad aim. His grandfather knew it, and when each shot went wide merely exhaled deeply and said "did your best, no man could ask for more."

Some farmer the century before had used his ax every twelve feet to notch limestone slabs marking Pastor Dale's property line. Still, after the third night of hearing the crunch of footsteps on snow, he decided to post his land. It took two hundred signs, and two full days to make an island of Ray's single acre.

Winter melted into spring, and one day the boy opened the storm door to the stoop to feel a warm breeze on his face. He looked down and, on the cinderblock stoop saw a paper bag with the top neatly folded down three times. Inside were four spotted legs, each sawn at the knee and ending in a tiny ebony hoof.

No one knows exactly what happened after that. Ray's truck sits in his driveway, now, tires flat and water reservoir dry. The curtains in his trailer are gone. The boy's mother fetched him back to Claysburg in time to start the new school year. Pastor Dale still fills his outdoor bins with dried corn mash, feeding the animals he'll track come fall. His pulpit's been empty since he stepped down. When people ask, he says it was him who did it, him who nudged his grandson's young arm. Who spoiled his aim.

How to Make the Squirrels Jealous
by George Choundas

When it's autumn and grim, the air like a clinic's, friends trusted and friends adored turn idiot. They spout nonsense about liking the four seasons. I got news. The third season is pure crime. Look, leaves. Every time the air moves, the ground seethes. Was there ever better proof of conspiracy?

When it's autumn and everything grim, the sky sere and withholding, the world is a great jar of dead things. My son and his laptop are loose in it somewhere, serious with ventures. My wife's at the stores hunting fresh turkey, talking about never frozen, talking about the pound-per-person rule, but they don't sell two-pound turkeys. What else to do but sit on a porch and make the squirrels jealous? I eat a thing like they do, in speedy nibbles with my hands hectic. It's a double business, my teeth the white worms plying a turd and my hands the dirty flies hectoring it. But I'll eat a massive thing like a double cheeseburger, or a personal watermelon grown in a different hemisphere. Or a meatball sub, because that was the special every Friday at the sandwich shop my father ran in the center building of a B-grade office park. Every Friday my father saved for me a meatball sub. He stashed it from the willowy receptionist who stood at the back windows in qiana polyester, smoking and gazing at the retention pond and declaiming in a high mastering tone things better for muttering—*He tells her I love you he has to but who does he call My love? who's the only one he calls My love?*—audibly enough to startle the other customers into hoping they were not the ones being addressed. He hoarded it from the mortgage brokers who proceeded chest-first as if every step broke a different finish tape and who demanded everywhere the specials because the specials in all of life's departments were their due. He hid it even from the pot-bellied doctor who grew shy tufts in his ears and spoke like a hippo with a toothache and kept a pious regimen for health's sake by ordering every morning a bagel because 1973 admired the carbohydrate like 1993 the opioid and 1953 the cigarette. The bagel doctor rewarded this daily forbearance by splurging on Fridays and going with the special but God help the good doctor if he showed after 2 p.m. because even chances that by then the only remaining sub knew sequestration for the proprietor's son.

What is love, after all, if not a length of fencing between the loved and the rest?

That sub would sleep the night in our home's refrigerator between the butter, moon-gouged and crumb-furred, and the juice. Only so many times a kid can eat a cold meatball sub without hating it. Not my fault, then, when I started giving away—in exchange for cafeteria spaghetti with sauce closer to sweat on a coloring face than proper blood—the sandwich my father made with his own hands and warded off the world from and brought home specially for me.

Just as well because who even remembers what side items he likes and doesn't like.

The squirrels stare at me with those near-sighted looks, at once piercing and wobbly, like a seventh-grader who takes off his glasses during lunch to look less bad when Laura Weller's sitting at the next table even though this means he can't really see her which may be the real reason because how do you exist successfully around a person as perfect as that? Their little squirrel chests rise and fall so fast it's hard to tell whether it's their hearts in awe of my haul or their lungs in anticipation of snatching it away. We stare at each other for a time. Then every one of them, every single one, scampers up, up toward that ashen disdain of a sky, up a tree or porch post, bushy tail trailing in conspicuous departure like the potentate striding across the tarmac who waves behind him for the clutch of snapping cameras but looks grandly ahead. This is how the squirrels console themselves. You may have bigger food, they think, and a bigger mouth to eat it with, but you fat useless lump can you do this?

I throw Cheesy Bits to the squirrels. I'm not a monster. The squirrels like Cheesy Bits.

When it's autumn and nothing but grim, this is how I console myself. You may have a faster metabolism and grippier toes, I think, but what kind of life is that, conquering branches and scraps, nothing dry when it rains, and you've never seen Laura Weller eat the meatball sub your father made, which is like eating a part of you, or heard her say, "This is amazing. Really. Thank you." I know two things: I wish the bagel doctor hadn't died of a heart attack years later in his own exam room but he did. And if you're jealous you should be.

Cranberry's Last Dance
by Sean Gill

My rusted Pontiac bounced from pothole to pothole and swung into the factory lot. Another overcast day, all dirty snow and no sun. In Northeast Ohio, pessimism is the great common denominator—hoping for sunshine on a winter's day is as fruitless as wishing upon a star, expecting a quiet lunchbreak, or rooting for the Browns.

I spent the next eight hours, as usual, caught between a jackal-faced motormouth named Darren Gempler and a bubbling plastic vat called a Sulfonate Goo Tank. My job was to fantasize about breaking Darren's jaw while keeping the tank safe and the drains clear. Captivating stuff, the soap business.

"I'm gonna kill Joe Cranberry," Darren announced, apropos of nothing. Even over the racket of the factory floor, his voice could needle, could *penetrate* the threads in your brain.

I looked around. No witnesses. "Why's that?" I asked.

Darren contorted his lips into a glistening leer. "Cause he's an old, gummed-up shitbiscuit sittin' on twenty grand, cash money."

Fifteen years ago, we attended Firestone High (Go Falcons), and Darren was a bush-league tyrant, the sort of kid who pulled the wings off grasshoppers and carved swastikas everywhere, for no apparent reason beyond the blunt shock of it. He hadn't changed much, though his ambitions (and collection of basement militaria) had broadened considerably.

"You got priors and live next door to him," I said. "You'd be Suspect Number One."

He wasn't listening. "There's foreclosures up and down the block. Nobody'll hear the shot."

"Well … that's good," I said.

*

Once upon a time, Joe Cranberry had been a boxer. Now he was a feeble old man living in a glorified garage on Spicer Street, surrounded by crumbling shingles and flaky salmon-pink paint. Darren claimed he was rolling in dough, but from what I'd heard, the palooka hadn't even clobbered his way past state lines—the best he'd managed was an undercard match (split decision) at the Richfield Coliseum. As I explained this, Darren doubled-down, insisting he must've made a fortune *throwing* fights. Darren never listened.

After a lifetime of having his brains beat into hamburger, Cranberry had gone demented. He lived life from an easy chair, silent and staring—unless there was a sudden loud noise, like a doorbell or car horn. At this, he'd pitch forward, find his feet, and put up his dukes. Somewhere inside that concussed skull, he thought the bell had rung and it was time for Round Twelve—*go get 'em, champ!* Pure muscle memory. Sad, really. An agency nurse showed up a couple times a week to feed him and change his diaper, but when she wasn't there, Darren liked to tap on the window and watch him stumble around through a slit in the curtain.

*

"It's a two-man job," Darren explained.

"To rob a vegetable?"

"I'm worried he'll put up 'em up—ding-ding!—when I break the window. Maybe those old knuckles got one last haymaker in 'em, ya know?"

"Sure," I said. "I'll come along."

*

Saturday night, the wind wheezed itself hoarse and the rain fell in icy sheets. The snow had melted, except for the densest, blackest piles, stacked up like little tributes to some unknown god.

The window was unlocked, so we wriggled over the sill and into his living room. Cranberry sat among the shadows, neck rigid, gaze fixed on the opposite wall.

"Hold this for a sec," Darren whispered. He handed me his pistol (heavier than I expected) and tiptoed beside Cranberry. Looming over him, Darren waved his hand wild. The old palooka didn't even blink. "Wouldja look at that shit," he said, amazed.

10

I was considering the hostility of noise and the right-eousness of silence when all at once my finger touched the trigger and a red rose blossomed at the center of Darren's chest. The sound came after. BANG! Cranberry sprung out of his chair and heaved his fists, knocking the empty carcass to the ground. Blood squirted on moldy carpet, how interesting.

I stepped over the body and uncurled Cranberry's knuckles. Carefully, I balanced the pistol's bobtail grip between his fingers. Seemed like a pretty open and shut case of trespassing and self-defense. I knew he couldn't understand, but still I told him, "Cranberry, hell—I believe you've scored your first T.K.O."

I called the cops from a payphone.

*

As I imagined how quiet my Monday morning was going to be, a peculiar sensation washed over me.

It may have been optimism.

"Cranberry's Last Dance" originally appeared in the "Mondays Are Murder" series by Akashic Books.

Roll and Curl

by Ingrid Jendrzejewski

It's a small town, so when a call comes through from Amber Groves for Mrs. Philips, you know it can mean only one thing: either her husband or her sister has passed.

"She's under the dryer," you say and pop your gum. You think you've made your point but end up having to add, "Well, you can come on down and talk to her yourself, or you can wait until I'm finished with her wash and set. We're in the middle of things here."

You put the phone down and look over at Mrs. Philips. She's under the hood dryer reading a magazine, lost in her plastic gown. She's shaking a little and at first you think she's crying, but then you see she's laughing. She has some lipstick on her front teeth.

When her timer dings, you remove the hood and check her hair. The gel has set, so you wheel her to your station and take out the rollers. You run your pick through what's left of her hair, teasing enough to make some volume, then comb the rest over the top to create the shape she likes. You form her bangs into curls by hand.

Then, you get out the hairspray. Mrs. Philips smiles, squeezes her eyes shut and lifts her chin. "This part always feels like spring rain," she says as you begin to spray.

You carry on for nearly three minutes; you carry on until you've used up the whole bottle. You spray until her hair is as hard as a combat helmet, until that smile is fixed on her face like a shield. Then you give her some tissues. You tell her they're for her teeth.

Pushing a Prayer

by Joy Kennedy-O'Neill

The prayers litter the surf-line, like plastic bags. Like clear jellyfish, or deflated bubbles. Bulldozers rumble on the beach, pushing them to the dunes. Some curl around beer bottles or a stray flip-flop.

Seagulls still laugh, as if it's the most natural thing in the world to have people's prayers drop from the sky and ride the Gulf's currents, bobbing on tides and turns and *Ave Marias.*

I pull on my work gloves. I don't want to touch them anymore. It's too much.

Dear Jesus Allah Kaddish *Om Bhur Bhuva Svah* Oh God our heavenly Father *Dios te salve, Maria…*

I tie my orange community-work vest around my chest, grimacing. Not from the shame of my DWI. But my left breast still hurts from the biopsy, and I think of the lump the surgeon removed. A grainy, sick, seed-pearl.

So what if I felt my mortality and drank too much, crashing into a CVS? I know, I could have killed someone.

Oh God, please let my lymph nodes be clear.

I look to see if I've made a prayer. Nothing. No cartoon balloon leaving my head.

I rake the prayers into the dunes, where the county says they'll shore up the beach. They'll mingle with the old Christmas trees, tangling up in strands of tinsel. Oh Tannenbaum. Maybe they'll help during the next hurricane.

Or not. The prayers are probably as useless as they were when they left someone's lips.

See, my weakness is that I don't have faith.

*

Three weeks ago, while walking Buddy, I smacked into my first prayer. I thought it was a spider web.

I pushed it out of my hair and heard, no, *felt* in my mind, "Oh God, please don't let Nana die." I saw worried people holding a wrinkled hand. I staggered on the sidewalk.

Buddy must have got the taste of one in his mouth, because he whined and offered his ball to a gleam.

They gleam a little, prayers. But they also clog cities' storm sewers and hang from people's gutters.

Catholics say it's a miracle. Lutherans say it's a trick. There's a joke about Baptists wanting to cook them up in covered-dish casseroles.

*

"Keep a positive attitude," my doctor chirped. I want to throttle him. So if my cancer spreads, it'll be my fault? Be-

15

cause I wasn't cheerful enough? Damn institutionalized victim blaming.

*

I come home and heat up a frozen meal in my silent house. It's awful to be scared *and* lonely. The guys I date are the type to freak out over the words "breast cancer."

I pray again. Hard.

*

I've never seen a prayer forming. No one has. In fact, the news says we may be sweeping up old prayers, or fake prayers, or a trick from North Korea, or pushing nothing. Maybe it's all mass hallucinations.

Journalists try to track down if some were answered, as other prayers get run over and stuck in wheels. Caught on fences.

People say it proves God exists. Others say the opposite. I mean, the prayers came back, right?

The cults say the end is nigh.

There are prayers of thanks. Prayers for forgiveness. You wouldn't believe what visions people see, when they grab a floating prayer.

I think of them glinting and roiling in sea-foam. Maybe global warming and the ozone layer won't allow them to float up to … wherever.

It's so obvious to me that there's no one up there.

*

Someone knocks on my door. It's a neighbor I've seen a few doors down, sometimes walking a beagle.

"Hi. This was caught up in my rose bush."

16

He hands me my prayer. It gleams a little. It feels like holding a wet baggie.

"Sorry what you're going through. If you need anything, let me know."

"How'd you know it was mine?"

He frowns. "I tasted your face. I mean, I *saw* your face. It's like—"

I get it. There are some senses we don't have a word for yet. "I know, it's weird," I say. "I've been on a city crew. We wear gloves."

"Yeah, it's so weird."

We both look at our shoes until he says, "Well, I'm around the corner if you need anything."

And I stand there with my sad prayer loose in my hand. Empty. Return to sender. It didn't even float very far. Have I been abandoned or answered?

Nice neighbor guy—I've already forgotten his name—turns around and waves.

And I hold up my hope-filled hand, waving back.

Childish Things

by Suki Litchfield

I was twelve years old the first time it happened. I was walking home from school alone, kicking a speckled rock along the road. Every time I kicked it, a puff of dust would come up.

I didn't notice the man until the rock skidded into his shadow. He was leaning against his black and white car, smoking a cigarette and watching me.

"You Lucia's girl?" he said.

I nodded. Everyone in town knew my mother. This is why I was walking alone.

"I hear she's away."

I said nothing. My mother went off sometimes, but then she came back. I was used to it.

The man took his cigarette out of his mouth and blew out a long stream of smoke. We both watched it rise up and grow thinner and disappear. Then he looked back at me. "You can talk, can't you?"

"Yes," I said.

He nodded. "I hear you take after your mama."

His uniform was clean and ironed, and the buttons and badge were shiny. I was wearing one of my mother's skirts held up with safety pins. The hem was coated in dust from my rock-kicking game.

"Thing is," he said, dropping his cigarette into the dirt, "that Atkins boy is still missing."

I had heard. The second graders were in the same building as us at school.

"See, I was looking for Lucia. But she's not around."

"I don't know where she is," I said.

He nodded. "I was thinking maybe you could help me instead."

I didn't know what to say. My rock lay a few feet away, and I bent down to pick it up. I don't know if the man thought I had tripped or was trying to get away, but he reached out and grabbed my arm.

And then I knew things about him. I knew his wife had black hair, and she cried a lot. That they used to have a baby, and when it didn't wake up one day, she screamed and screamed. And that there was a blond girl in town who he liked to see naked.

When I straightened back up, I looked the man right in the eyes. He pulled back his hand like I was a hot stove.

After a moment I said, "I was getting my rock." I opened my hand and showed it to him. It was covered in dust, but you could still see the speckles and the bits of mica.

"I'll help you," I said.

I went around and got in his car. The seat was comfortable, and he didn't say anything when I cranked the window open. When he did start to talk, it was about the Atkins boy, about the sweater they'd found, and how he sure would appreciate any ideas I could give them.

I looked out the window and squeezed the rock in my hand. I liked how it was hard and jagged, but glittery if you knew how to look.

Review

by Sue Showalter

I recently went to this restaurant with my husband because we read about this restaurant in a magazine and so we made a reservation on the date of May 18 and upon being ushered to our table I noticed that the table was wobbly and near the back of the restaurant though the water placed on the table was very cold and I enjoyed the fact that we were given a pitcher of water as I hate having to request more water because I like to drink quite a lot of water while I eat.

When the waitress arrived she immediately asked if we wanted something from the bar and why she would presume we wanted something from the bar I don't know and after explaining that we wanted water she walked away and I noticed that her skirt was too short as this young woman is employed in this restaurant that we read about in a magazine but she's wearing a skirt that shows approximately 14 inches of thigh and she's approximately 19 years old with no stockings assuming everyone wants cocktails and bending and leaning and laughing over plates of food and I clearly saw saliva spurting from her mouth into a large bowl of soup.

In addition this waitress was wearing a shade of cotton candy lipstick that one wouldn't associate with this restaurant that we read about in a magazine and had clearly thrown her hair into a slapdash ponytail probably following days of not showering throughout various fraternity parties in which she was paraded around in a matching cotton candy boa to then come to our table and show her teeth and lean over the table in a suggestive way talking about specials as if we came to hear about specials after reading about this restaurant and knowing exactly what we wanted to order in advance of our May 18 reservation.

I continued to drink my water and was very happy that we received a pitcher of water as I hate asking for more water but then the water was empty and the waitress did not return she did not inquire about the status of the water but instead laughed and joked with other members of the staff in this restaurant that we read about in a magazine as we waited for more than 30 minutes for our food which in another restaurant would seem reasonable but I suspect the delay was due to this waitress's unprofessionalism as demonstrated by the skirt and the lipstick and the laughter and the bending and leaning and the showing of teeth.

After finishing our food the waitress returned and said something along the lines of isn't the food delicious as if we needed someone to tell us the food was delicious as if we hadn't read about this restaurant in a magazine and knew the food was delicious but she assumed she assumed we thought it was delicious and did not bother inquire about the status of the water despite the fact that it was now only 1/4 full and had lost its satisfyingly cool temperature so at this point in the meal I lost my own cool so to speak and I told this waitress in this restaurant that we read about in a magazine that she was disgusting and should not be employed in this restaurant in a magazine as our meal in this restaurant that we read about in a magazine had been ruined by her horrendous skirt and her failure to check on the status of the water as I hate having to request more water because I drink a lot of water while I eat.

This waitress in this restaurant that we read about in a magazine then requested the assistance of a manager who said that he was respectively requesting our departure at which point I articulated my refusal to pay the bill at which point he insisted on calling the cops at which point I grabbed the waitress by the ponytail and pulled her to the floor which from a distance seemed very clean but was riddled with some kind of crumbs maybe sesame seeds though I don't recall any sesame seeds on the menu and as I delivered appropriate blows to the ponytailed head of this waitress in this restaurant that we read about in a magazine I reiterated the problems we encountered i.e. the lipstick and the saliva and the skirt and the bending and leaning and the unattended water and why would she assume we want something from the bar not everyone wants something from the bar.

And as I continued to deliver appropriate blows to this waitress in this restaurant which was a restaurant that we read about in a magazine I recalled that things haven't been that great lately but I won't get into that now just know that they're terrible and so we read about this restaurant in a magazine and thought we should go to that restaurant in the magazine and show our teeth and drink our water and go home and wallow in a spaghetti-filled sleep in which things exist in a way that you forgot as you got older and you can feel the wonder of being a child and seeing a big open field and running into it and the joy that feels like sex but it's not sex because you're a child and everything exists without any conflict or sadness or doubts or insecurities or questions about God and death and money.

So as you read this and you think about the lipstick and the skirt and the bending and leaning and that unattended water and my experience at this restaurant that we read about in a magazine I hope you can understand that I enjoyed the fact that we were given a pitcher of water as I hate having to ask for more water because I like to drink quite a lot of water while I eat.

Ode to a Bee on the Small of Your Back

by Partridge Boswell

Blind to what tickles the delta of nerves there
you rub a humming with the back of your hand,
surprised by the soft pulse of a drowsy bee

that somehow hitched a ride on your chambray shirt
when a moment ago you went outside, barefoot
in cool October dew to kiss your love goodbye

through her driver's side window beside late
rugosas that waited till now to speak, each petal
speckled with a hundred glistening tears of sunlight.

Winter still counties away, larkspur fooled by
recent heat into blooming again, the meadow
rue still tall, its edges only beginning to tinge

like an iconic actor with a full bucket list of roles
to gray into. The garden and hive you tend for another,
thriving these six years (or is it seven now?) since

she left. Easy to lose count with sun's wheel grinding
memories smooth as it fades needles and leaves.
Easy to see numbers for what they are: cold

and stunningly meaningless as stars. Easy to say
winter would have killed him anyway, as you bend
and lift him from the kitchen floor with a spoon.

"Ode to a Bee on the Small of Your Back" originally appeared in *The
Gettysburg Review.*

Pit-Stop Sisters

by Threa Almontaser

At Khalu's gas station, we lizard up an 18-wheeler,
latch onto the ledge to see who can grip it

the longest. Our contest since leaving the womb:
who can rival truckers with the dirtiest

trash talk. Spit wads into the farthest bucket. Be brave
as a motorcycle & ride with the biker gangs. I have peach

fuzz I'm proud of. She finds a few hairs on her armpit,
so we're even. I get extra points for smelling like diesel

& lifting tires without quivering. She takes the lead for
hitting Khalu's hookah pipe, her bison coughs, shrouded

in berry smoke. These boy things, these men things
halted as Ama sifts our scalps, steel teeth stuck

in my sister's 'fro. Each tug splits us, our eyes
tear-glints. *Scritch scratch* in the apartment that smells

of Moroccan oil, meat cleaned & cut on the counter.
Aha, my aunt tuts. *Crack* between her fingers, little flicks

on the floor to sweep later. I wonder how buried
the tiny nits are. Eggs glued to the white line

of my skull. If one will escape Ama's ruthless hunt,
insistent itch, legs climbing out the sac, follicle feelers

crawling for me. Ama won't let us cut it. Every day
is a nest untangled, thick sheets to our tailbones.

Tea tree, garlic, lime—kitchen cabinets pilfered
to kill. She goops cold remedies onto my head,

irons curls that demand an audience. She is a hot
wind at our necks when she says, *God chose long hair*

for girls. If you cut it like a man's, you'll be cursed.
& yet. If I were born a boy, I'd have an animal

slaughtered, a sacrifice added. My head shaved,
anointed with saffron, gold given out equal

to the weight of it. My furrow cupped, foreskin
sliced off, celebrated as bloodied & clean.

Boys drive around the neighborhood whistling
out the sunroof. We watch from the window—

exposed skin, shorn hair. & there we are, clamped
between Ama's thighs, being clutched by the fistful,

ensnared like crickets caught in the yard, their tireless
clicks in her hands. At night, I feel my chest swell,

scared I'll wake to the shape of a woman. A body made
to be entered, carry babies, a soon-to-be wife. I'm losing

big time now. I press them down, pray to prolong
my boyhood. & for my dad's knuckles, rusted black

from tinkering. The strength in his fists. Broad back.
A penis—all of it passed along like an inheritance

or a cold. I dream I chop off my hair. Wind power
from a speeding car blows the long strands away.

Compulsory

by Derek Annis

I don't remember what it was—losing
a game, or some form of hunger—that made me
pick up the hockey stick and chase
the neighbor boy across the lawn. Whatever
it was, I wanted to kill him—to pack his teeth
tight against the back of his throat
with that stick. He was ten. I was eleven,
and I loved him. Together,
over several summers,
we sat beneath every tree
in the forest, walked every inch
of the river. We even tested
the infamous French Kiss—I let my tongue slip
into the moist cave of his mouth,
and enjoyed it
for a moment, before rearing back

at his stagnant taste, the popsicle
stickiness of his lips. Once, while hiking,
we wandered too far. The sky went black
and fell into the forest, we were off
the trail. There were eyes, and snapping
twigs. Matt began to cry, so I swallowed hard
held his hand, lied about knowing
the way home, and said all the wolves
were sleeping. It was after twelve
by the time we crossed
the front lawn, found our parents
sitting on the steps with bitten lips. Mine engulfed me
in warm arms—carried me quietly
up to bed. Matt's mother
slapped him—dragged him inside
by a fistful of hair.
Hands want what hands want:
lead the scared boy home
through the dark,
bring the stick down hard
on his tender face.

"Compulsory" originally appeared in *The Meadow*.

Leaving the Garden

by Tom Boswell

You knew this day would come,
didn't you? Turning over the soil
for the last time, remembering
routines that never seemed routine.
The double-digging a decade
or more ago, the soil never the same:
too moist, too dry, at times just right.

How you turned it over and tucked
the voracious earthworms back in,
recalling once more that it's just
a myth how they heal miraculously
when sliced in half with the shovel,
and now you hear your heart insist
no creature can expect ever to be whole
again after losing something so precious.

How you tossed the stones and walnut
shells on the path, and here you are,

still fishing rusty nails and shards
of glass out of the dirt, stuffing them
in the back pocket of your jeans.
All the shovelsful of compost, peat
and manure you sprinkled in the beds
while robins waited patiently nearby,
knowing there would be worms for lunch.

Sometimes a toad was exposed
and you sent him on his way with a nudge
of your finger. Once you uncovered
a nest of baby rabbits. One of them,
too small or scared to move, huddled
there all night on the garden path.
In the morning, you watched a crow
swoop down and carry it off.

The cedar waxwings came again
last month, gorging themselves on berries
of the red cedars with no thought
that providence might ever fail to provide.
And the resurrection lilies by the pond
rose once more, out of the dark, in a burst
of glory, and you marveled at their blind faith.

Now it's late October, still warm,
and the birch trees are clinging
tenaciously to their last few leaves.
Your greenhouse is gone now,

just a dark blemish on the ground
where it once sat. A would-be farmer
with dreams of plump red tomatoes
hauled it away, battered though it was
from the time the storm snatched it up
and tossed it on its side.

Hastily you harvest a few beets and carrots
and leave the rest in the ground–soon
to be frozen–recalling the years of labor,
the love once fresh, now wilted.
A mother of the new couple comes
to inspect the house and eyes the vase
of flowers on the kitchen counter,
vibrant purple coneflowers and
black-eyed susans from the garden,
and she hands them to you, saying
"They won't be needing this."

How can she say what they might need?
you think, but you take them, a bittersweet
gift for the first person you meet
on the street, because it hurts too much
to hold on to them, and you walk out,
you walk away, and don't look back.

Handstitch

by Carlos Andrés Gómez

I am holding my friend Gino's hand
and asking the army recruiter for more
information—*About the Marines, please*
I say. He fidgets with his cuff links,
paws at his first communion crucifix
through his shirt, drags the back
of his hand across the close-shaven
sandpaper of his chin. Gino is staring
him down through the eyeliner he wears
like a middle finger. We watch this stranger:
caught between the trained movements
of a machine and the churned butter
in his body. Just like mine, two months
before when I said *Hell no* to a trip
to the gay club. *I just don't want to lead
anyone on. It'd be like colonizing the space*

I said. Which sounds a lot better than
I'm uncomfortable. I wouldn't know
how to stand. What do I do if a song I like
comes on? In East Africa, I walked
the dirt roads of a township, my pinky finger
intimately wrapped around the smallest
digit of the most infamous guy on the block.
He was my friend. It is how friends
walk the streets there. When I greet
my Iranian friend's father, we embrace
cheeks twice. In Thailand, my host casually
patted my leg at the first family dinner.
I nearly jumped out the window, thinking
he was reaching for something else. Everyone
laughed. A passerby gives me and Gino
matching names. I tongue the word around
in my mouth. Feel the tender sting make
a home in my torso. Stare at the word
Brotherhood splayed across a camouflage
banner. The recruiter stares down
at the table, as though it holds the secret
code to life's great questions. His corrected
stutter and slightly overcompensating
stance blend into the decorations behind
him. So much so that I can barely even
tell he is still there. He pretends we are not.
Begins sorting and re-sorting the three
lonely pamphlets dwarfed by the large
rectangular table where they now sit.

Boys, seriously. I'm just doing my job.
Please—his mouth begs in a voice
so small and human it makes me
feel like I have just blurted out
a secret this man has given his life
to guard like freedom.

"Handstitch" originally appeared in *Chorus: A Literary Mixtape*
(Simon & Schuster, 2012).

Constellation of Bones

by torrin a. greathouse

the forest curves around me tightly as a scalded palm, skin
   peeling
into clouds slumped low enough among the trees to be
   mistaken

for mist, or a gasp of steam from the valley floor—spread
   wide
as a newly vultured corpse—its edges clung with the last
   wet suds

of yearling snow, like curdled milkfat or maggots dreaming
   gut-heavy
against a deer's caved-in breast. there is a wind chime
   dangling

in the mist. closer, no. not a wind chime. though it's limbs
   percussion
into a fevered tune. the sides of its throat applauding into
   the absence of air

between them. the wire circles its vein-thick neck like a
   maypole. the goat
hanging, ornamental, limp as a storm's decline. its eyes fat,
   pink, & pitted

as late-season plums. each pupil a single gouge, a thumb
   nail splitting
peel. even now, how pulseless the knowing: that i will leave
   its body

strung into the air. imagine the flesh sloughing away, bones
   suspended
as salt in brine, or constellation—pinholes in the blue-bleak
   fabric of night

—& how i long for such animal knowledge: to invent of the
   sky an exit,
a doorway in the wind, breath swung open on the hinge of
   the jaw;

to see in the body a room & know how to leave it behind.

"Constellation of Bones" originally appeared in *Waxwing*.

Washing Red Leaf Lettuce

by Margaret Koger

Hold the head under a faucet
Feel water streaming through the leaves.
Pray for the leaves of your family.

Twist the rosette until stems rupture.
Use two hands to hold loosened leaves.
Recall shadows from last year's eclipse.

Check the sink for grains of sand.
Balance the head while you rinse again.
Sing a chorus of house built on a rock.

When satisfied the once nurturing soil
Has drained beyond all reproach
Reflect on the desertification of the planet.

Spread the lettuce on a clean towel.
Wrap the fabric into a tube and press.
Remember drying a baby's tears.

Unroll the tube and open the folded leaves.
Admire the core's white heart.
Lament the burden of your secret sobriety.

Rewrap the lettuce, coax to dry, free the leaves
Refrigerate in plastic and hang the towel in the sun.
Remember—*all things* are never equal.

Monday Nights at Michigan's Only Women's Correctional Facility

by Isabel Mae

*t**he only place i feel safe*, she says *is in my fingers while i'm crocheting.* we all nod, there's nothing else to say. her sister, a cop, 15 years no talking finally asked her what it's like in there

i want to know where it is i'm sending these people.

what absurdity to write in a line. what divergence, what spider web of silence, so damn sticky. these people, these women in blue. these posters in the hallway of the programs building screaming

SMART IS SOMETHING YOU BECOME, NOT SOMETHING YOU ARE.

how to read that? who chose these words to break the silence? *yeah he's done for* she laughs, *got caught with an in-
mate's mouth on his dick in yard 2, behind the dumpster.
made her*

lick his badge. notice the words we use to name ourselves.
notice how easy it is to turn into object, perpetrator, vesti-
bule, whatever the sentence needs. noticing adaptation.

NO ELEVATORS TO SUCCESS, TAKE THE STAIRS.

i want to know where success is a building i could summit,
we all nod, *i want to know who built it, how steep*

they made my stairs. a woman born from a womb in the
center of a cell, her mother's

arms still shackled, legs opened for necessity, balancing on
the shoulder of another woman

born in addicted blood, born already a comrade of death,
the two of them in the center of our classroom practicing
movement, how to construct ourselves in time and space,
how to take up

more time and more space

how to say the apologies, the unconquerables when they've
sat in ribcage too long, gathered

43

dust and look like clumps of hair caught under the couch.
when they're screaming *please*

just sweep us up together and throw it all away.

Surrender, She Said

by Steve McDonald

I was kneeling like a devotee before the sprinkler valves

the ones that unfurled the flow of water to the backyard
where years earlier you had celebrated the liturgy of fescue

Kentucky blue & rye though this day the yard was all

yellowing grass & tenacious weed the faded black valves
themselves old & cracked two still working two not

all of them half-buried in the sift of dirt the wiring rotted

as well as the encrusted plastic levers that once allowed you
to turn the life-giving water on & off by hand so I knelt

knees scraping the fractured gray concrete surrounding

the narrow pocket of soil from which the bonnet
of each valve rose into the ragged line of my vision

paper towels tucked like a stole into the collar of my shirt

to shield my neck from the lick of summer sun I was wet
with sweat exhausted not because the labor

was so Sisyphean though it seemed it was but because

I knew you wanted the grass to grow the way it once did
when you could walk its myrtle-green in your gesture

of sky-blue blouse open at the neck & white capris

& to be honest I wanted that too so I dug deep
into the packed soil with a pick & trowel to lay bare

the pipes that led to & from each valve I told myself

I was doing this because it would please you though
the truth is the tendon & sinew of the job which were really

your desires made flesh were themselves deeply satisfying

I slid the saw one inch in one direction & one inch
in another it was slow work my right wrist bled lacerated

by the jagged edge of concrete it scraped against

but soon I was lost in the sawing & bleeding & sweating
the back of my neck on fire as if touched by an open finger

of flame & before I knew it I had become the dirt

that stopped the saw the concrete that scraped the skin
the riser that resisted every pass of the saw's teeth

it was as if I'd spun into the pipe itself resisting any change

no matter how painful the cut & isn't that the way it is
resist & persevere resist & outlast resist the way men resist

resist the way *life* resists never give up so how is it one word

you offered me bending over my shoulder as I struggled
in the middle of my life your ringed fingers touching

my back how is it your one whispered word delivered me

"Surrender, She Said" originally appeared in *Cimarron Review.*

in conversation with yet another therapist i stopped seeing

by Bailey Merlin

*F*rom the beginning, please.
My mother told me she loved me
with Christmas sweaters in July.

I am throwing her ashes out to sea,
but the wind keeps sending her back.

I remember Leila. Did she find
what she was looking for? he asks,
making notes on how I hold my hands.

Listless as ever, I change the subject
and tell him that I micro dosed molly
at a Latin club last night just to feel
a little more lotus and a lot less mud.

The comedown was a real sonofabitch,
but it helped me hang onto the ribbon
threaded through my brain, in one ear
and out the other, dredging up childhood
when a guy in another blue button down
asked me to dance, his smile gin-certain;

I wanted to know if he had an MBA.
He did, and I said, Color me surprised.
I'd rather color you mauve.
I couldn't decide if this was a come on.

There's a box of tissues on the table
that my fingers make short work of,
strip after strip. I want to make myself
scarce. He's a pendulum. My ribs are
constricting then expanding out larger;
there's not enough room, so I let it out:

Do you think Lazarus's resurrection
made him happy? Or did he spend the rest
of his preternatural life trying to get home?
Suicide is a sin, you know; death, a sacrament.
Do you still have the sweaters?

Of course I do but don't admit that I've unraveled
them into piles of knots that are hidden in my house.

They didn't fit me anymore. *Maybe it's time
to give them away.* His words linger there,
ash in the wind, blowing back into my face.

The Voice of Someone Other

by Robert Murray

The Lord hates a coward—that's what
my father used to say, when he was alive
and wide-eyed, nodding, beckoning me to jump
from the end of the dock into shivering Otty Lake.

Strange turn of phrase, always seemed to me—
he who never once breathed a word of God
except when belting it out, hardily, heartily, even
beautifully from a back row pew in the United Church of

Something-Or-Other that my mother dragged us all to
for a while. Slight, timid man in character, I never saw him
stand so tall as with hymnal in hand, feet planted
firmly on a freshly waxed floor, singing from his toes

and heart and soul, my savior God, to thee,
how great thou art, how great thou art.

Where did that come from, I always wondered,
but never asked. The voice of someone other than

who he was, no doubt—a man without the inner
wherewithal to stand up to his wife and say No,
these kids don't need to be here in a stuffy church
on this clear spring morning, and neither do I.

How I hated those Sundays and his cowardice,
forever attending to her needs instead of his own
and mine. I wasn't about to sing, oh no, not a chance
of that, left the hymnal mute in the rack and stood

only to give my ass a break from hard wooden seat.
But not singing made it worse, cause then I couldn't
help but hear the passion in his voice, all that raw feeling
and the way he seemed to come so vigorously to life

out of a dead sleep. Reticence, that's the word
I used years later, describing the thing that lives in me
that I hate most. He said, Yes, consider that part
of your inheritance, like a battered old chest of drawers

nobody wants and even the Salvation Army will refuse to
take off your hands. Then he touched me on the shoulder
and squeezed, just a little, a kind of invitation, it seems
to me now, said, Our cross to bear, Son, wouldn't you say?

And today I would say, want dearly to say Yes
to that cross we still bear together, to trust
it was bequeathed to both of us for good reason,
and trust it's okay to regularly still feel

like that scared two-year-old teetering at dock edge,
knowing that if I pause, summon, and leap
that his outstretched arms and the glorious eruption
of thunderously jubilant praise await.

Revenants

by Claire Scott

They come at dusk
    Aunt Eleanor baking cinnamon bread
the sweet smell of anticipation
Uncle Sam in the corner doing the weekly
crossword puzzle, winking at the child
I once was
Nana smiling a gummy smile that says
there is a pink sucker in her purse
Mother sloshing scotch
reciting Shakespeare sonnets
what of my friend Carlene bringing
scraps & shreds of shiny gossip
or Richard with an armload of roses
stolen from his neighbor's yard

my children are alarmed
make an appointment for me with Dr. Robert Stein
who prescribes pills to take away the specters
says in three days they will disappear

I toss the pills in the trash
sit by the window &
wait for dusk

On the Anniversary of Your Infidelity

by Leona Sevick

Moving around the bed, stepping with delicate feet
on every uneven surface, he settles finally on a place
behind my knees, curling into a tight, breathing ball.
Soon he'll begin to snore, and on trips to the bathroom
or to the dresser where we've placed glasses of water
out of his reach, we will move gingerly, careful not to
hurt him with our clumsy bodies. To think I once
considered boiling him in the pot I use to make soup.
Because you love him, too, I thought I might just
gather him up in my arms, let him lick my eyelids
with his flypaper tongue, sniff his fertilizer smells
one last time before dropping him into the boiling water
and closing tight the lid. I got the idea from that film
I saw on my very first date. The boy who took me,
it turns out, was damaged, too, and I wonder if he ever
thinks back to the dark theater smelling of popcorn,

his hand gently resting on my knee as we watched
the girl find the empty rabbit cage just as Anne Archer
opens the pot. I should have known you can't watch
a thing like that and expect to live happily ever after.

"On the Anniversary of Your Infidelity" originally appeared in the
poet's anthology *Lion Brothers.*

Train at Night in the Desert

by Amie Sharp

Georgia O'Keeffe, 1916

Georgia, it's been one hundred years
since you stood in the dark Texas dawn
and marveled at the multicolored haze
clouding toward you down the track.
You thought the rest of your life
would unspool from Canyon, Texas.
You wrote Alfred Stieglitz that you saw
the train, thought of him, and blazed.
You had never even been to New Mexico.
I think of you, so young on the stark
gray sand, in the path of the oncoming,
which looked that night like a train,
glittering alive and black,

its light fixed upon you
like a sun, like an eye
seeing what no one else can see.

"Train at Night in the Desert" originally appeared in *Burningword Literary Journal*.

When I Was Straight

by Julie Marie Wade

I did not love women as I do now.
I loved them with my eyes closed, my back turned.
I loved them silent, & startled, & shy.

The world was a dreamless slumber party,
sleeping bags like straitjackets spread out on
the living room floor, my face pressed into a

slender pillow.

All night I woke to rain on the strangers' windows.
No one remembered to leave a light on in the hall.
Someone's father seemed always to be shaving.

When I stood up, I tried to tiptoe
around the sleeping bodies, their long hair
speckled with confetti, their faces blanched by the

porch-light moon.

I never knew exactly where the bathroom was.
I tried to wake the host girl to ask her, but she was
only one adrift in that sea of bodies. I was ashamed

to say they all looked the same to me, beautiful &
untouchable as stars. It would be years before
I learned to find anyone in the sumptuous,

terrifying dark.

Little Emotions

by Mary Wolff

*Let's not forget that the little emotions are the great captains
of our lives and we obey them without realizing it.*
—Vincent Van Gogh

The strange man in the living room calls me baby
and tells me to be a good little girl and go hide.
The corners of his mouth rise up and down like sangria
in the pitcher being carried by my still beautiful mother.
She spills and steadies herself a moment
against the edge of a chair. Her mouth is a perfect circle
of breath pushed out with distant force.
Has she been saving that breath for years?

Our cat pissed in my bed when I was little.
My mother scrubbed it with her small fists, but the smell
clung to the room. I woke up every morning
wanting to peel back the layers of my skin
until it smelled like lavender and limes.

Limes and salt
on my skin years later as a sweaty stranger
takes a shot off my shoulder. His drunk dry tongue
scratches like sandpaper and up rise familiar smells.

Tequila.
Smoke.
Piss.
The cologne of a certain kind of man
a woman would rather forget.

Palloncino

by Lauren Lynn Matheny

The boy was holding a balloon. That's what everyone could agree on—he'd been walking along the edge of the wall, atop the soot-stained balustrade, and he'd been holding a red balloon.

No, a pink balloon, said the man who sold arancini at the cart near the entrance of the park.

There was no doubt it was blue, from the woman who'd been walking her bichon near the fall.

The little girl who'd been swinging on the derelict old swing set (which the town council had been rallying to remove for several years now) said that the adults were all wrong, that the balloon had been the color of raspberries when you mash them into the bottom of your bowl, and that she had gotten a splinter from the swing seat.

Whatever the color, there had been a balloon. There had been a boy. And there had been a fall.

The sky had turned its eight thousand shades of crimson and purple, before it happened. Really, everyone agreed, it was too late for children to be out at the promenade (this, with a judgmental glance at the little girl's mother, who was rumored to be no better than she should be). The working men had cleared the streets for their dinners; the babies were in bed, dreaming their sunset dreams.

Someone, though, had not understood the meaning of conscionable time. Someone had allowed their son to play out on the city streets, to play atop walls, to slip at the place where the stone grew slick and mossy.

In the absence of any other information, they agreed that the child must be an outsider. Any of their children, should they be atop the balustrade in the first place, would never skip on that particularly traitorous stretch of stone, knowing full well that the sea air hummed up off the rocks below to create a damp and slippery sheen just there, next to the third bench of the promenade. Any of their children would understand the inherent risk of holding to a balloon, one hand incautiously distracted; they would surely never walk without two feet and full focus planted firmly on the narrow beam below them.

The butcher's wife, who had not seen the fall but who had come by at the sound of commotion, had been heard to cluck distastefully—her husband knew the chief of carabinieri, who'd said that the boy had been dressed in cheap wool shorts and a ratty old cardigan, with a tiny cap on his head. Shorts, in the middle of *October*; all she could say was that no child of hers would be seen in the middle of winter, half-dressed.

Or, it was to be presumed, walking on top of a balustrade, with no one to watch him, said the florist, who was known to be a particularly spiteful man.

That goes without saying, sniffed the butcher's wife, before remembering a prior engagement.

The florist's daughter, as it happened, had been the first to come upon the crumpled little body, broken on the shoals under the promenade's walls. She'd been boating with her paramour, ignored his horrified protests, and steered them to the boy. When the more sentimental members of the crowd asked if she'd attempted resuscitation, the practical florist's daughter had replied simply—it was obvious that no efforts in that direction would be needed, since the boy's skull had been crushed in by the rocks.

She did not relay that she had, in a moment of unusual sensitivity, plucked the little boy's hat from where it lay perched on a rock. She imagined it had floated down after him, taking its time to descend, whereas the boy's body had plummeted in no time flat. The hat was well-mended and sturdy, the sort of thing you'd find in an old antique shop.

The police had inspected the hat for any identifying details, and found none. When they'd turned their backs to address the medical officer, the florist's daughter snatched the hat from the table and shoved it in her purse. It was illogical, of course, but she suddenly could not abide the thought of the lonely little hat sitting, bagged, in a cold evidence drawer.

One young police officer, new to the force, had had the brilliant idea to canvas the balloon sellers in a two-mile radius; the buoyancy of the thing, as reported by spectators, ensured that the balloon could not have traveled far from its origins.

The balloon sellers, to a man, claimed that they had sold no balloons to a child of such description, poor little tyke. October was not a brisk time in the balloon trade. They also found it unlikely that the child would have bought a balloon and inflated it himself; when this tack was suggested, they smirked knowingly at the carabinieri, as though these starched shirts would never have any idea of the mystery and the majesty of their trade.

Only the florist's daughter was left to think, that night, after the boy's body had been cut open and investigated, his description posted on flyers and news alerts, his little form locked safely away in a drawer and tucked in to sleep under a paper blanket, at the ugly truth of it all—that the juxtaposition in the sight, the boy's body tumbling through the air and the flight of the balloon, tinted fire-heart red by the last flicks of the sun, up into the half-shadowed sky, was one of the most beautiful things she'd ever seen.

Bargains

by Margaret Adams

The problem was, there never seemed to be a good day to try to kill their daughter, no matter how many safeguards were in place. In the doctor's office, a week after she had been discharged from the hospital, it had seemed like a good plan—a fine plan. Allergy testing was expensive, more than an eight-hour drive away, and anyway, the kid got carsick on the old dirt logging roads. *We're not sure why Grace's airway swelled and stopped her breathing*, Doc Hamilton had said to them, but another way to figure it out—besides driving all the way to Boston for the fancy testing—was to spend a Saturday in the cracked plastic chairs of the small community hospital waiting room and give the girl everything she'd eaten on the day she'd stopped breathing. But slowly, component by component, with a few hours between each thing. Scientific-like. *Bring a Monopoly board with you*, Hamilton had said. When the troublesome ingredient caused her airway to swell, she'd be right there, not an hour away at the gray-shingled farmhouse by the mill. The Emergency Room staff would inject her with epinephrine right away and it'd be fine.

Outside of the doctor's office windows, the sun shone down on the snow banks, making the gravel and road salt embedded in their dirty surfaces glitter. Dave and Sally, still thick with the early, heady dizziness of their daughter's survival, had nodded eagerly, shaking Doc Hamilton's hand. A fine plan, they agreed, we'll just go on a day-trip to the Emergency Room—it'll be like a family science day. A science project! *Except a short one, sweetheart, once we figure out what you're allergic to—they'll treat you immediately, it'll hardly be five minutes, they won't even have to cut your clothes off this time, though to be sure, it's probably best not to wear the new pink shirt with the bunnies stitched on it that day. Maybe wear the old hand-me-down from your sister with the Kool-Aid stain. We'll go soon.*

But the right day just never seemed to come. It was either too nice outside, or they were too busy, or it was too close to her birthday.

Dave remembered the way Grace had looked the night she'd stopped breathing. The small pale oval of her face turned upwards as he'd thrown her into the front seat of the Chrysler he'd always hated. He had sped towards the lights of town, driving as fast as he could, headlights illuminating the patchy reflective lines on the otherwise dark and wooded roads. Maybe he could have driven faster if he'd still had the old Dodge, but maybe the Dodge wouldn't have started—it often didn't—and—a thousand *what-ifs* and *if-onlys* and *please-God-nos* had welled up and threatened to throttle him as he drove, a choking panic, even as a very real invisible fist clenched around his daughter's tiny throat. She'd panted and yanked at the seatbelt, fighting the flat nylon webbing as if that were the force keeping her from taking a full breath. She'd stopped whimpering before he'd gotten two-thirds of the way there, quietly turning a slow and delicate blue, clawing at the velour seats with increasingly less frantic hands. He'd gunned the Chrysler across the lot, parked in the fire lane and carried her in through the doors labeled "Emergency" in wide peeling red letters, yelling *she's not breathing* in a voice unlike any he could recall coming out of his throat before.

That night Mark Eisley had performed CPR on Grace for four minutes before the epinephrine worked. As Mark said to Dave years later, misjudging a moment of camaraderie during a drunken hunting season cookout as an okay occasion for a medical confidence, he'd only kept from breaking Grace's ribs because she was so young that her ribs were still as much cartilage as bone.

When she'd lived, it was like a new lease on everything, the *what-ifs* all landing butter-side-up and the *please-Gods* answered for no discernible reason. Dave wondered, privately, what he had bargained away on that drive, what promises he'd made and debts he now owed for Grace's life.

He caught himself cautious now, not for new disasters—surprisingly, he and Sally still let both of their daughters eat dirt, let them play in the rain too long, hollered *go take a long walk off a short dock* when they were underfoot—but cautious for the bargain he felt in his bones that he must have made. He eyed unexpected choices askance, wondering if this was the deal he must have made that night come home to roost. Had he exchanged her life for the O'Brien's offer on their back acres, swapped a prayer in the night, and was now meant to listen, and give the man the lot for an unreasonably low price? Or was the twinge starting up in his left knee meant to stay forever and worsen, a plague of the bones he'd accepted as compensation for those four minutes of CPR that had worked? He wasn't afraid, exactly, and never—not-ever— regretful, but he wanted to know his fate when it came, to see head-on the bargain he fancied he'd made. Wanted to own the machinations that had thrown their family into a wire-crossed intensive care unit for three days before spitting them back out again, still whole.

Doc Hamilton's plan had felt like a good one. There just never seemed to be a good day to go through with it, not even in the name of science and with the antidote on hand. They were afraid, but they didn't want to admit it, not to themselves or to each other and certainly not to Hamilton. And so a month went by, and then another, and then twelve years had passed and both girls were grown, Rachel off at college and Grace graduating from high school. They never had made it to that community hospital waiting room, never figured out the cause of Grace's near-demise.

Our weakness kept us from doing what we needed to do to help her know her own enemies, Dave thought. *The soft damnation of love.* "Once in 18 years isn't bad odds," Grace joked when the topic came up, and a finger of cold ran down his back. He laughed, but shifted one leg to the next. Grace looked at him sidelong, not knowing that the specter of her blue face had just passed before his eyes. "Is your knee bothering you again?" she asked. "You're standing funny."

*

Hamilton was the same doctor who did Dave and Sally's marriage counseling. He was the same doctor who prescribed Sally "post-natal vitamins" for two full years after their youngest daughter was born before the pharmacist finally let the cat out of the bag by calling and telling her that the refill on her antidepressant was ready to pick up. To Dave's surprise, Sally didn't seem to mind, though it did clear up a few questions about why the second daughter's infancy had been so much easier than the first's.

Hamilton was also the one who had said, "Have a beer when you're breastfeeding," when Sally had called him up frantic that Rachel didn't want to take her milk. "It'll calm you down and make it easier." It had worked, and if a little beer got through to the infant, well, that probably calmed the baby down, too, and wasn't it true that their own mothers had stuffed whiskey-soaked handkerchiefs in their mouths when they were little?

Rachel had been born seven months after Dave and Sally's town hall marriage and five months after they'd moved up north so that Dave could take the job at the mill. While Dave had been out of the northern counties for three years, people thereabouts still remembered him, and if the bride he brought back north was an out-of-stater, well, at least she was an out-of-stater who had the sense to marry a Pendleton. Sure, he'd left, studied starry-eyed at a down-county college where he'd lost his belief in the written word, met Sally, gotten her pregnant. But then he'd come back home, just like they had known he would. Dave was a good man for the job, especially since he'd gained a little cynicism around the edges. Not too much—that would be unbecoming in a man with a new wife and a baby, even a County man—but enough to make him more dependable.

Rachel was born on a gray January day at the end of a three-week string of gray January days. They were in a shared Labor and Delivery room separated by a worn curtain from a young-sounding woman who screamed, over and over again, "I don't want to have a baby! I don't want to have a baby!" until the labor and delivery doctor, impatient, yelled back that she should have thought of that nine months ago.

Dave fainted during the last few minutes of the delivery around the time that the doctor had cut Sally "just to make a little extra room for the baby" and had a woozy memory of coming around in a chair to the sound of his first daughter testing her lungs. Sally wept. A nurse placed Rachel in Dave's arms, and he thought, not for the first time, about what a joke it was that they took making decisions so seriously, as if they could possibly have any reasonable idea of what they were getting into in life before they were actually there.

In the weeks that followed Rachel's birth, Dave drove Sally and Rachel back to the clinic for check-ups with increasing frequency. Sally sat silently in the front seat of the Dodge, holding the baby's diaper bag on her lap, staring out the window. Outside of the car, three-string barbed wire fences encircled the frozen wave-like tufts of late March hayfields, undulating clumps of straw so cold that you'd think you could grab a fistful and break them off, but which actually resisted any form of destruction, yielding instead to worn boot heels with a near-soundless crunch.

At the clinic, Sally moved the baby clothes and spit rags around with slow hands that seemed disconnected from her body, while Dave sat next to her, back straight, inarticulately desperate.

"The babies mostly grow fine on their own," Doc Hamilton confided later. "It's the parents we need to see every four, eight, sixteen weeks."

Eventually, the woman Dave had married returned. One week Sally started showering unprompted, no longer had to look at her hands and arms before doing anything as if to remind herself of their uses, and began making sardonic jokes again. As for Rachel, she had grown—grown well, if a little clingy, which, given everything, was understandable— into a toddler with corkscrew pigtails and a grave sense of humor. Dave drove Sally and Rachel around on Sundays, and when the Dodge wouldn't start, they thought it was funny.

Some days Dave would catch himself in moments of happiness so simple and intense that he would become afraid, because he knew he had done nothing even halfway notable enough to deserve it.

Sally had always planned on a second child, but after several years of trying, they'd begun to wonder if the first early accident was going to be their only one. Just as all expectation was beginning to fade, the hundredth home pregnancy test came out positive. To Dave's great bafflement, instead of celebrating, Sally, who had done plenty of bargaining of her own, locked herself in the upstairs bathroom and refused to come out for three days.

"I don't want to be pregnant," Sally said through the closed door, her voice thick. "I can't go through that again." And then nothing, just the occasional sound of the tap being run.

Dave read the same book out loud to Rachel twenty-three times, let her wear her rain boots all day, and brought her down to the Boucher's General Store for hot dogs and ice cream cones. Together they arranged plates of sardines and Saltine crackers for Sally and left them outside of the bathroom door.

"We haven't seen Sally lately," Eloise from next door said as Dave stood at the end of the driveway, considering the mail that had built up. "Is she doing okay?"

"Well. Yes." Dave paused, looking up at the dormers of the house rather than directly at his neighbor. "The thing is, she's pregnant."

"Oh," Eloise said. She looked expectant, waiting for him to say more.

"She's in the bathroom. She hasn't come out for a few days."

Eloise mistook this revelation for a description of severe morning sickness and not Dave Pendleton's wife's latest existential crisis. "Has she tried ginger tea?"

Dave began leaving mugs of ginger tea outside of the bathroom door along with the plates of sardines and saltine crackers.

When Sally emerged from the bathroom on the third day, she got in the Dodge and drove straight to Hamilton's office. Her appointment lasted a full hour. When she came home, she set Dave's keys on the counter, knelt and hugged Rachel hard, inhaling the hair at the nape of the child's neck. Then she went to the attic and brought down the cardboard boxes of baby clothes that had been folded away years earlier.

Dave wasn't sure what exactly was said in that office, but he didn't ask. The first time, with the first, unexpected pregnancy, they had talked about it. But after the loneliness of Sally's pregnancy and the wretched despondency that had followed, Dave had grown cautious of asking her questions if he wasn't sure he wanted to know the answers. In a way, he knew, her depression had been his fault—his child, his job, his northern county. So while he, too, wanted a second child, he said very little, and when Sally emerged from the doctor's office, still pregnant and newly resolute, he said nothing at all.

There were five inches of the first snow of the season on the ground when Dave drove Sally carefully through the streets to the hospital. The birth was shorter and easier this time, in a room with actual walls. Afterwards, Dave wheeled Sally outside so that she could smoke a cigarette in the pale winter air while the nurses cleaned and inspected their new daughter.

The child, Grace, had all of her fingers and toes. Always, this was the thing that the parents checked, anxiously, eagerly, as though the number of fingers and toes somehow insured that everything else would be okay, that the first trimester whiskey really hadn't done anything wrong, and everything was fine. The not-fine things, if there were any, lay dormant and without portent. They knew this, but still they counted, and then told everyone, *ten fingers and ten toes,* and everyone replied, *thank God,* though they, too, knew that it meant nothing.

*

Dave believed in the calculus of life, a vague sense of arithmetic that had been neither explicitly articulated nor discouraged. "One good turn deserves another," was something his father had often said, not always cheerfully, tallying up what they did and did not owe their neighbors. Dave understood that some things in life were trade-offs, either/ors, exchanges made and tallied.

In the hospital the night Grace had stopped breathing, one of the nurses—a traveling nurse who staffed rural hospitals for six-month stretches of time—had looked sternly at Grace and said, "You have been very, very lucky." Grace had dimpled and yawned, having already made the swift shift from terror to boredom with the restoration of her breath, but Dave knew that the nurse had spoken to him. *You have been very lucky.* It felt more like a threat than a benediction.

He'd seen the nurse once more after Grace had left the hospital, carrying a grocery basket through the aisles of the Boucher's. He'd wanted to approach her, but hadn't been sure what to say. *"Thank you?" "Take it back?"* It wasn't hers to take back, and he wouldn't want her to, anyway, but she was the only person who'd understood that a bargain had been made, *had* to have been made, that Dave now had outstanding debts to the universe.

*

"How long can a kid go through CPR, and come out of it totally okay, like Grace did?" Dave asked.

Doc Hamilton eyed him from behind his wire-rimmed spectacles, not questioning the non-sequitur. The two men were in Dave's office at the mill, talking in the aftermath of another worker-injury on the floor. As the foreman and the family doctor, they often found themselves here, sweeping up the sawdust and blood together. The paramedics had come and gone—County had an ambulance service now, one which, he'd been told, would go all the way out to their farmhouse now if they called—but Dave had called up Hamilton out of habit, and he'd arrived at the mill not long after. A half-filled out incident report lay on Dave's desk; both men had been bent over the pages of the paperwork, their sleeves rolled up. In knit caps and wool sweaters, it was hard to tell who was who, the medical man and the mill supervisor.

"It can be surprisingly long," Hamilton said. "For kids under seven, to come out okay, it can be up to 6 minutes, anyway. Kids under three can lose their airways and keep a pulse—stop breathing, but still have a heartbeat." He straightened his glasses. "It's different for adults. Adults, you lose your breathing, you lose your heartbeat too. It just happens like that."

Dave nodded, then continued to fill out the paperwork.

He had been given the Chrysler by the mill's upper management after the first time he'd cleaned up after an accident like this. "You handled that well, Pendleton," he was told. "People trust you. And you show them they can." He remembered the fervor he'd felt for studying journalism, the intoxication of righteous truth, and then the disillusionment that had come with seeing the ways in which even truths could be used to manipulate. Before the Chrysler had been given to him, he would take short breaks, work through lunch. Afterwards, he began taking the full hour for himself, reading paperback novels held one-handed with the covers bent back around their spines, eating his lunch slowly. No matter where he sequestered himself for those long lunches, there always seemed to be the tickle of sawdust in the back of his throat.

He thought about leaving the mill, but as the girls grew, those thoughts came less and less often. It was steady work, and Sally and the girls needed that of him. He wondered at what point indecision became a choice, avoidance the address you gave.

By his forties, Dave's hands had taken on a dry, chipped look. The changes happened slowly, nicks and abrasions causing an almost geological ablation of callous and sinew. His wedding band and his grandfather's watch had worn indentations, deep grooves accommodating the metal. When the girls were small, they would wrap their whole hands around his fingers and hang on with a strength and boldness that astonished him. Later, they would learn to hang on to their loved ones with less directness.

As the years went by, Dave still carried with him that uncertain sense of something owed. He'd seen some debts paid—injuries on the mill floor, the foreman whose job he'd taken so many years before, the delicate balancing of the scales of chance. He remembered every petition he'd sent out into the universe: to get out of his town and go to college, for Sally to be herself again, for Rachel to grow into a healthy child despite their struggles. For Grace to keep breathing the night he'd sped toward the hospital chanting *anything, I'll do anything, just let her live.*

There were so many risks Dave hadn't taken out of fear of unbalancing those murky debts. He never asked Sally the questions that might hurt, as if the harm would be lessened if it were not spoken of out loud. Questions like, *are you happy?* Better to help her pretend that everything was okay. The unasked proliferated between them—imperceptibly at first, then with a growing weight which muffled, like a permanent embankment of snow.

*

Two weeks after she graduated from high school, Grace was in Dave's workshop, helping him go through boxes. She worked efficiently as she sorted through his old college things. Dave often wondered how it was that Grace and Rachel came out the way they did, so fully formed, so separate. There was a face both girls had learned to make, an artful expression that could be interpreted in any direction the viewer wished to perceive it. He'd watched them turn that face on their mother, admired how it had worked, not recognizing it as his own. On Monday, he and Sally would be driving Grace south to Hampshire County, where Grace would be enrolling as a freshman, like Rachel had before her. This time after they returned home Dave would be moving into an apartment not far from the mill.

While Grace sorted books, Dave wrapped up the tools that constituted his domain: the old family rifle that he carried through the woods every fall without ever firing or even loading. A dusty box of unused cartridges. The percolator, stained black from years of being filled and emptied, purchased during bachelor days and relegated to the garage.

It was quiet in the workshop, and Dave realized he'd stopped hearing the steady rustling of Grace moving his things. He looked up to see her sitting cross-legged on the ground, an open box in front of her, stacks of papers arrayed in a semi-circle. He recognized the reams of writing he'd produced in college—his words, marching out in print, as bold as her childhood hands wrapped around his fingers.

"What is all of this," she said, not looking up from the papers splayed under her hands. He couldn't remember his own hands looking so young. "Dad," she said. "What's this?"

"Grace," he said. He cleared his throat, the sawdust feeling following him sometimes even here. "I've been thinking. Let's head south a day early. Stop in Boston and see that allergist," he said, "remember, the one Hamilton mentioned years ago?" He paused, his hands on the rifle he'd never loaded, packed now under a layer of waxed cloth. "Don't you think it's time?" He said, his voice rising, gaining strength with the question. "Don't you think, now, before you start school?"

"Bargains" originally appeared in *Pacifica Literary Review*.

Like the Leg of a Y

by Katherine Ayars

The girl knows that he means what he says this time. She can detect patterns and, this morning, the pattern was different. This is why she knows that today is the beginning of the good days. Joseph usually says, "I love you. Don't leave." But this morning he said, "I love you. *Forgive me.* Don't leave."

Forgive me. Yes, of course she forgives him. But she must be careful. She must not change her routine just because he has altered his.

She creeps to the bathroom without a sound. It's as if waking the dog will somehow alert Joseph. She opens the cabinet beneath the sink and withdraws a writing tablet. It sits atop seventeen others the same size. They're all full, every last page decorated with her left-handed letters and numbers. As she exits, she catches her reflection.

Her nightgown is old, but she refuses to part with it because it reminds her of the first few weeks with Joseph. He had phoned one day while she was ironing his teacher outfit, and he had said that the vision of him and her living like man and wife had given him an erection. Though she wasn't supposed to, she had gone out that afternoon and spent twelve dollars. The pharmacy sold pretty nightgowns in pastel colors and she had had her eye on one with flowers and swirls; the design was soft and happy like a baby's birthday cake. It was short, unlike her other nightgowns. She never wore clothing cut too high or too low; she just wasn't that way. But she had suspected the little housedress would please Joseph. And it had.

The pen now rests more comfortably in her left hand than it did at first. Four months ago, she decided to train her brain to think in a new way. She has read that right-handers use their left brain and she wants to learn to use the right half instead—the half that the world's most innovative people use. Henry, who works at the store and sells her the pads of paper, says, "That's a bad idea." He says that she is charming the way she is and that she is in danger of changing her personality if she changes around her brain. Henry is old and wise because he has seen war, but she does not listen. She is a soldier with a clandestine mission, and she will see it through.

Joseph doesn't know about the eighteen pads, but he doesn't need to. Each day, as soon as he kisses her goodbye and closes the door, she practices her letters and numbers. She had a dream recently that told her to keep at it because the day she is able to form perfect figures is the day that Joseph will ask her to join him in matrimony. They will have a quaint outdoor ceremony. She will carry lilacs and wear no shoes and she will use her left hand to feed him a bite of cake while everyone watches. The guests will whisper that he is a lucky man. She will have a new last name and a newly developed brain, and everything will be right in the world. But she is not in a hurry; rewiring one's mind is not a task one can accomplish overnight.

She doesn't have a job because, for a few years, she was in a relationship with a man who had a big fancy house and had asked her not to work. Not working her waitress job was fine with her because it made this man feel like a hero.

Joseph, too, wants to feel heroic, so he lets her stay home. And it's okay that his house is small and unsophisticated; she needs neither porcelain nor crown molding. The breakfast nook in this little house is flooded with sunshine and she can't think of a more perfect spot to build the dolls. She is crafting a collection that she hopes to sell in the general store. The dolls have special eyes. They're not those sneaky eyes that try to follow you around; they're eyes that look straight to one spot with a promise that won't be broken.

Beethoven's *Eroica* fills the room. She is proud that the pattern has been carved into her brain, but it hadn't been easy. Joseph had yelled about her not being able to hear it, but as soon as she had listened alone, it all made sense. Slow, slow, slow. Fast, fast, fast, fast, fast, fast. She is embarrassed that it took her a few listens to pick it up. But she knows if she does what he says, she'll be a better person. Like with the shoes. Joseph taught her that taking them off without unlacing them causes them to break down twice as quickly. He also made her understand that vodka is cheaper than wine and that most people can't smell it on you. Another bonus is that vodka doesn't make you feel like you're still on a Ferris wheel the morning after.

A. B. C. One, two, three, four, five, six. Her hand doesn't cramp like it did weeks ago; it's strong now. She fills every line on seven pages because that's how many bites Joseph took to eat his eggs and cheese toast this morning. Then she replaces the pen's cap and looks in the pantry so that she can plan dinner. He likes to eat chicken and cabbage and those tiny potatoes on Tuesdays, but this Tuesday is not like the others. She wonders if mixing up the menu will alert him to the change he has initiated; she doesn't want to wreck things by creating too much variety. She closes the pantry and takes the package of frozen thighs out of the freezer. Then she washes her hands with scalding water and soap.

She changes into pants and Joseph's old oxford and leashes up the dog. Their neighborhood once seemed unfriendly, but that was back when she lived alone. She used to like running into him when she went on strolls. He found it endearing that she walked even though she didn't have a dog, and she thought it was silly that his black dog Buford had a white spot on his chest that was way down low. It was as if his tuxedo jacket had been unbuttoned after a long night of revelry.

The first time she ran into Joseph, she noticed that his pants were wrinkled and that they were too short. This convinced her that he did not have a wife. Or if he did, the wife did not know how to properly tend to a husband. When Joseph first told her his name, she said, "That is my favorite name. I've always known that if I have a son, I will call him Joseph."

"Don't laugh," he said, "but I find your name remarkable, too. I'm a fan of the Russians and Anna is a name they often employ."

She didn't know what he meant by "the Russians," but she knew that he was smart. He was a Music teacher at the high school. She couldn't imagine being so brainy that people would pay her to shape kids' minds. She had worked hard growing up but her father had realized early on that she wasn't made to be a surgeon or a lawyer or anything.

He had encouraged her to work on her personality and pay close attention to her looks. She has this funny scar shaped like Greenland in her eyebrow and because her hair is dark, and her skin is light, the scar is pronounced. This flaw has always bothered her father. He tells her it happened the time she fell out of her crib, but she thinks that story is boring. She imagines that as a child, a Greenlandic pixie branded her in the night because that's where she would settle with her husband. Her father had taken her to the make-up counter when she was young so that she could fill in the flaw. "You have to maximize your potential if you want to have a husband and appliances one day," her father had said. "Symmetry is important. It makes one look capable."

She was a very good listener and she had always listened to her father. But she stopped filling in the scar once she was on her own. She hadn't planned on it; it was just one of those changes that creeps up like a coffee stain in the kitchen sink. Slow and steady.

That's how her walks are. Slow and steady. She is patient and now knows how to handle a big dog. She lets Buford lead her to the right. This is the sign that he wants to go on a walk she calls *I am with you*. She named it this because the pattern involves walking straight into the sun on a slight incline; and, being blessed by the ray's direct warmth reminds her that she is not alone on this journey.

She stays out with Buford for twenty-nine minutes because that's how old she is, then she heads up the front walk. She loves walking the same straight line that Joseph walked only four hours ago. She can feel his presence and she thinks that she can even make out his footprint.

When she moved into his home last year, he confessed that he would return from their street corner encounters and think of her while touching himself. She knows that some women might find this degrading, but she finds it romantic, especially because her ex had called that type of behavior "oddly voyeuristic." He was older and very serious and had often said, "You should never do anything you wouldn't do on the steps of a courthouse." She loved him a great deal, but she had always had this feeling that she'd be lost if he left her but found if she left him. She didn't want to live her life on the steps of a courthouse. So, she packed her bags and left him a note.

Buford loves returning from walks because it means that it's time for a treat. She is allowed to give him only one even though he would like to have two. She once gave him an extra and that night he yacked all over the sofa. Joseph was so mad that he hurled her hairbrush at the bathroom mirror. She was pretty scared, but when it was all over she wasn't angry; she knew the episode had occurred for a reason. The shattered mirror meant that she wasn't seeing herself straight, and the brush's broken handle was a sign that she should cut her hair like he had asked.

She washes up and gives Buford a biscuit. Then she repositions the pen in her left hand. Her letters are jittery, which is not normal. She knows that this is because things are changing. Things are being pushed and tossed and flipped all around. And as soon as everything settles, she will be transformed; she will be a blown-glass butterfly. Joseph will see how delicate she is, and instead of dropping her, he'll place her high on the shelf among his best records. She'll become one of his rare first editions—flawed but beautiful.

She has forgotten most of the damaging words, but some things won't go away. This is the problem with loving a man who speaks well; he knows how to say things like, "You are my sky, my all." But he also knows how to say, "All you've ever done is keep a billionaire's bed warm." Her ex is far from being a billionaire, but she knows that Joseph isn't great at math even though he's smart enough to never end a sentence with a preposition. She also knows that molding the minds of children requires heaps of patience and sometimes Joseph is plain tapped-out by the time he arrives home. Like what happened yesterday.

A co-worker had gone to Joseph's class to listen to the kids play the violins and the clarinets and the cellos. After the mini recital, the co-worker had taken Joseph into the hall and had told him that kids aren't stupid; they can smell off-gas. The worker had said, "You should consider having your last drink at six p.m. instead of six a.m." The co-worker doesn't know that statements like this make Joseph drink more than his usual share.

The extra vodka last night had inspired Joseph to carry a kitchen chair into the garage and bash it against the wall until his hands bled. She had listened to the destruction from the safety of the kitchen and she had recited the alphabet from A to Z and Z to A until it was all over. He had cleaned up the mess and everything was fine. And he hadn't actually thrown anything except words. Statements that didn't make sense and weren't directed at anyone in particular. Statements like, "You don't know about blood" and "All I remember is that there was a white dog."

When Joseph unleashes the gibberish, she doesn't say anything back. This makes him even madder, but she doesn't have a choice. Her mind just goes too dizzy to talk. It's as though the thoughts are being tossed round and round in a dry cycle and all she can hear is the loud "shhhhh" of the machine's exhaust. She knows that sound is the world telling her to keep quiet and still. When this happens, Joseph takes Buford out and after about an hour of cooling down, he returns, showers, and climbs into bed.

Joseph likes to make love with the hall light on. She doesn't understand why because he isn't able to look at her when she's on top of him. "I have to close my eyes or I'll come." This is what he says every time. She rocks back and forth for a little while and whispers when she's ready. Then he opens his eyes and stares at her breasts and they come together.

She slides writing tablet number eighteen back into the bathroom cabinet and says, "This is just like making love. We will now come together in new ways."

She sits at the table with her paints and basket of dolls parts. The arms and legs and torsos are together on one side and the heads are on the other. She fishes out a head with brown hair and readies a paintbrush. She knows that this doll will have green eyes because last night Joseph listened to Schubert's *Unfinished*, one of his favorites. The number of letters in Schubert is eight; and, in the case of evens, doll eyes are colored green. When Joseph listens to someone with an odd number of letters in his name, the eyes are blue. And when he listens to nothing at all, the eyes are colored brown.

She blows on the doll eyes and sets the head down to dry. She can't believe she has spent so long on this one pair; Joseph will be home soon. She knows that things are different now. Better. But she wants to be sure. She must find a way for Joseph to tell her without words. She turns on the hot water and lets it run over the still-frozen chicken. She thinks and waits and thinks some more.

Then she feels warm, so she showers. While she is soaping herself, she takes the empty cup from the shower caddy and fills it with water. She uses it to rinse the shower walls; he hates it when her stray hairs cling to the tile.

After she steps back into her clothes, she combs her hair with the brush that is now missing its handle. She thinks it's funny. The brush was once long like her hair, but now it is cropped like a bob. She has an idea. She will cut her hair. If Joseph notices the change before he pours his drink, then her suspicions will be confirmed; today will indeed mark the beginning of the good days. If he doesn't notice the cut until after the drink, then she will know that she has been wrong about it all. She will accept that she and he are a cloud that is pulling itself in opposite directions, and she will pack her bags and leave him a note.

She takes the scissors in her right hand and a clump of wet hair in her left. She closes her eyes then cuts. She knows dead cells can't feel, but she can. A row of miniature dominos lining her insides begins to topple. They start at her ankles and fall all the way up her spine. Faster and faster. Across her skull and down her arm bones. She opens her eyes and cuts. And cuts. And cuts.

Joseph was right; she does have a nice neck. She imagines that today he will come home and kiss it. He'll skip the drink and take her straight to the bedroom where they will come together like two raindrops that slide down a window and move into each other to form the leg of a Y.

She hears the door open. "Anna?" he says.

She rushes to greet him.

He kisses her forehead. "You showered. In the afternoon?"

"Yes. I don't know why," she says as she follows him into the kitchen. She knows her feet are moving; she can see them. But she can't feel anything except a scarf of air looping around her neck and shoulders.

He washes his hands and the steam fogs his glasses. It clears as he opens the freezer. She leans her hip against the counter for support. He removes the vodka bottle, the ice tray, then a glass. She runs her fingers down the back of her wet bob. He takes three cubes from the tray and anoints them with spirit. "You look happy," he says, "as if…"

"As if what?" she says as she leans harder into the counter.

"Tell me why you're smiling," he says, and he grins too.

"It's…"

"It's what?" Then he takes a sip.

She slides her palm along the counter that she will never know after tonight and says, "Nothing. It's nothing at all."

Orange Crush

by Karlyn Coleman

The dying were restless in the morning, so I started helping out around the hospice the year I turned fourteen. I refilled pitchers with water, delivered mail, and opened the sliding glass doors to let in the scent of sand and sea and damp eucalyptus leaves.

When I was seven, my mother quit her medical practice, quit with the saving of lives and began to focus on the terminal, turning our Malibu home into a bed and breakfast for the dying. *House of Peace,* it was called.

The house sat just off the Pacific Highway. It was made out of glass and white concrete, long and lean, wrapped around the tip of Dumas Pointe so that every room had an ocean view. My father had designed the house that way. He wanted the house to feel as if was floating in that space between sky and sea.

"Avery, you need to finish what you are doing and get ready for school," my mother called to me as I was about to deliver a vase of flowers to a patient at the end of the hall.

Standing near a window in the morning light, I could understand how patients sometimes mistook my mother for an angel when she came into their room. She was a tall, slender woman with long, shiny black hair and eyes such a light blue they looked silver in bright light. Patients never mistook me for an angel. I was scrawny and pale with hair the color of dry sand.

Ghost-girl, was what the kids at school liked to call me, because not only did I live in a place where people came to die, but I was also the whitest girl in Malibu.

The California sun had killed my father. I was six when a mole, hidden under my father's thick strawberry-blond hair, turned indigo blue. The cancerous roots spread quickly through my father's skin and bones and laid a nest of tumors in his brain. Six months later he was gone.

"I've asked Edith to drive you to school," my mother said flipping through a patient's chart. "I have a lullaby I must begin."

When it was time, my mother gathered family and friends around a patient's bed and helped lull the dying to the other side.

Tell them they can go. Give them permission to leave. Forgive them. Love them. Let them go.

Sometimes, the dying went quickly.

Gone.

But other times, it took hours and sometimes days.

Stalled in the labor of death, my mother called it. She was fascinated with the similarities between birth and death. *A Doula for the Dying* was what she called herself then.

"Who is leaving?" I said surprised. I was sure no one was going to die, not that day. I had discovered that I was really good at predicting death. I could predict not only the day, but the hour when someone would pass.

"Mr. Solece," my mother said in a hushed tone.

"Mr. Solece?" I said. "He's not going anywhere."

I was sure of this. I could smell death before it came. And it was not a foul scent, but syrupy and fruity and sweet. I smelled it for the first time when I walked into my father's hospital room the day he passed. I sat holding his hand and could smell the sweetness of his life escaping, bubbling up in the air. I just didn't understand what it meant, not then.

Death, I tried to explain to my mother just a few months ago, *smells like an orange soda going flat.*

But my mother told me that what I smelled was the build up of ketones in the body, a sign that the kidneys were shutting down, but it wasn't just that. It was something more. My power of smell was remarkable. I could close my eyes and inhale the air and know not only who was standing next to me, but if they were happy, sad, angry or full of fear—the scent of lemon blossoms, salt, sour milk, burnt toast.

I couldn't remember the sound of my father's voice anymore, but I remembered how his hands smelled of graphite and ink—how when he held me in his arms, his love smelled of strawberry ice cream.

"Why don't you believe me?" I said when I saw the way my mother was looking at me.

"Because you have not gone to medical school," she said as she turned from me and began to head back to her office to make her phone calls. "Because you can't know such a thing. It is only the last beat of the heart when we know someone is gone."

I didn't argue with her, because I knew that if I did, my mother would think that I couldn't handle working in the hospice over the summer. She wanted to send me off to a camp in the Sierra Nevadas, but I did not want to go. I hated that camp. I had never felt more alone in my life than those six weeks I had spent there the summer before.

Patients at the hospice often reached for my hand and asked me to sit next to them. I felt the importance of being a part of the good bye, whispering in their ear when I knew they would go—*you are loved, you are loved, you are loved.*

"Edith will meet you outside," my mother said as she disappeared into her office. "Please don't be late."

But instead of delivering the flowers and going upstairs to get ready for school, I stepped into Mr. Solece's room again. I wanted to be sure, so I stood next to his bed and inhaled the scent of him.

"What time is it?" Mr. Solece said slowly opening his eyes, looking at me.

"After seven," I said because I did not know the exact time. There were no clocks in the rooms, no clocks in the halls. My mother thought it was cruel to have patients watch the minutes and hours of their lives tick by, but they were always asking for the time, always wanting to know.

"Morning or night?" Mr. Solece said looking out his window. The morning fog had not burned off yet so the sky was heavy and grey.

"Morning," I said.

He looked at the flowers in my hands.

"Are those from my Leonard?" he said reaching out is arms towards them, and I didn't have the heart to remind him that Leonard was already gone. The dying often forgot who was living and who was already dead.

"Yes," I said setting the vase on the small table next to his bed even though the flowers were for Mrs. Jenson, but she had so many, and Mr. Solece had none.

"Is Leo here? Has he come to visit me?"

"Not today," I said, taking Mr. Solece's hand in mine. "But soon."

Mr. Solece nodded his head and closed his eyes and I sat for a few minutes with my hand in his.

"Avery," my mother said stepping into the room. "What are you still doing here? You are going to be late to school."

"Sorry," I said and ran up the back staircase to our small apartment upstairs and changed into my school uniform.

On the way outside, I broke off a stem of lavender and shoved it up my sleeve. The smell of a something picked from the gardens outside was the only way I survived all the smells that surrounded me at school.

Edith was already waiting in my mother's Saab.

"You are going to be late," Edith said.

"I know," I said as I opened the car door.

Edith was my mother's assistant. She helped with all the patient's paperwork and insurance forms. She was a wide-hipped, wide-shouldered woman who took great joy when she was asked to leave the dying and run me around to be with the living.

"I'll remind your mother about your band concert tonight," Edith said nodding to my clarinet case.

"It starts at 7:00," I said, but I knew my mother probably wouldn't make it. She had a hard time leaving her patients. She promised each of them she would be there at the very end.

"You don't mind if I take the top down," Edith said as she pushed a button and the top folded up and behind us, revealing the misty, California sky above.

"Just drive fast," I said covering my head with the hood of my jacket to keep my fine, hair from getting tangled up in the breeze, but it didn't matter how fast she drove, I knew that the first bell at school had already rung, and that once again I'd be late, and there was no way to explain to the attendance lady, to anyone, that it was the dying, the constant stream of dying who kept me from getting anywhere on time.

*

I was given a detention for my tardiness, and after school I was forced to sit in a small room filled with a dozen other students. The room was warm and filled with the scent of boredom and stale fruity gum. I put my head down in the crook of my arm and inhaled the scent of lavender and the pages of the paper-back book I was reading, but the scent of sour-apple gum kept creeping in.

A girl started to laugh behind me and then another, and when I reached and touched the back of my hair, I felt the warm stickiness of chewed gum. The more I pulled, the more it became entangled in my hair.

I got up and ran to the restroom and tried to get out, but I couldn't, and spent ten minutes washing my hands with pink soap that smelled like wet cardboard and then tied my messy, gum-tangled hair into a pony tail.

"How was school?" Edith said when she came to pick me up that day.

The radio was blasting tunes from the 70s and Edith was smiling, so I didn't say anything about the gum in my hair as we drove along the coast. I just asked her about Mr. Solece. I wanted to make sure he was still there.

"He's had a turn about," she said. "He was sitting up in his bed having tea with an old friend when I left. Not ready to go. Not today."

I smiled at this. I knew I had been right. It was the only good thing that had happened that day.

When we pulled into the long, black drive, an ambulance was parked out front. That was how most of the dying arrived—transferred from hospitals when nothing else could be done—sirens silent, lights off.

A young girl, not much older than me, stood by the ambulance's back door. She wore bright pink sweatpants and an oversized T-shirt. One of the paramedics handed her a backpack. It was red and there were charms hanging off the back, glittering in the sun. I did not stay to watch the paramedics unload the patient. It made me sad when people arrived, because I knew they would never go home.

Hotel California was what Mr. Solece called the place when he first arrived.

I went up to our apartment and took a shower and covered my hair in conditioner, but the gum still did not come out, so I went in search of my mother.

She was in her office, but not alone. I saw the back of the girl sitting in a chair just in front of my mother's desk.

"We will make him comfortable. Come with me, we'll get you both settled."

The girl stood up and with one hand she picked up her backpack, the charms jingled together and tinkled like a miniature wind chime.

"How long do you think he has?" she said. "The doctors at the hospital thought just a few hours, but it has been five days."

"His heart is strong," my mother said. "Nurture him. Love him. No one can say. Just love him and take it day by day."

When the girl turned around, I saw that she was holding a tiny baby wrapped in a yellow blanket. The baby's head was covered with a knit hat, but I could tell that his head was not normal, it was too small and his eyes were not right.

"Avery," her mother said when she saw me standing in the hall. "This is Julia and her son Oscar. They will be staying with us."

We had never had a baby in hospice, a child of any kind.

"Hello," I said trying not to stare at the baby.

"Hey," the girl said as she rocked the baby in one arm, and tucked her thick, black hair behind her ear with her other hand. She looked like she was in high school, about sixteen, but her eyes looked older—brown irises tinged with grey.

A nurse led them to their room.

"I may be delayed tonight," my mother said after they were gone.

I put my hand to my hair. The gum was woven tightly in the back.

"My concert," I said.

"Oh, I'm so sorry. I've made arrangements for Edith to drop you off on her way home. I need to get Oscar and Julia settled. I promised an old colleague I would take care of them. The girl has no one. No one at all. Her last foster family kicked her out after they found out she was pregnant. A child dealing with the death of a child. Your father led them to us. This is why we are here. We have to do all that we can do to make Oscar's last days as beautiful as we can."

I said nothing. What could I say? Julia, a dying baby, my dead father—they trumped my band concert, they trumped everything. I showed my mother my hair and she didn't even ask how the gum got there, but picked up her phone to make an appointment with her hairdresser.

They couldn't get me in until the next day, so I ended up tying the matted hair back into a pony tail and waited for Edith to gather her things and give me a ride, but this time we drove in her car, an old yellow Honda Accord that smelled of stale coffee and old french fries.

Edith parked her car in the parking lot.

"You don't have to stay," I said.

"I want to," she said. "Love a good concert."

"It won't be exactly good," I said.

"It will be great," she said walking me into the school.

At the end of the concert, I saw my mother standing against the wall.

"You performed just beautifully. Lovely," my mother said, so I knew she missed my solo, missed when I knocked over my music stand, missed the way the first few notes squeaked out of my clarinet.

"You didn't see it," I said.

"I'm sorry," my mother said as we drove back home. "I tried to get there on time, but we needed to find a crib and special equipment and formula for Oscar."

I didn't say anything. I just watched the moon reflect off the white-capped waves as we drove along the coast.

When we got back home, my mother checked in with the staff and I walked around the garden out front. Before I even saw Julia sitting on a bench, I caught the scent of her cigarette. The ember of the cigarette glowed then faded, and then glowed again like a lost lightening bug.

"Hey," the girl said to me as I approached.

"Hey," I said sitting down beside her.

"You live her?"

"Upstairs," I nodded to the second floor.

"Is it weird?" Julia said and then flicked her cigarette to the ground, stomping it out as she walked towards me. "Living here, I mean."

"Yeah, it's weird. Weird to live in a place where everyone dies," I said and then felt bad for answering so sharply, so coldly, I had forgotten for a moment that she wasn't a kid at my school, but that she was there because she had a baby who was dying too.

She lit another cigarette.

"I smoked before I knew I was pregnant," she said when she saw me looking at it. "I stopped as soon as I knew."

I nodded at this.

"You want one?"

I'd never had a cigarette before. "Thanks," I said as she handed one to me. The cigarette was nearly weightless between my lips. I let it float there, not lighting it. I could smell the tobacco. It smelled like the wet reed of my clarinet.

Julia inhaled and tilted her head up towards the sky. "But now, I mean, God, no one would tell me I can't smoke, you know."

"I'm sorry," I said, because I knew that was all you could say. There weren't any other words but, *I'm sorry. So sorry.*

She handed me a purple lighter and I tried to light the cigarette, but it kept going out, a tiny trail of smoke stinging my nose.

The side door the hospice opened and I could hear my mother talking to one of the nurses.

"I should go and be with Oscar," Julia said.

I nodded and started to head to the side door that led up to our apartment.

"You should stop by and see him. He's like holding a doll," Julia said.

"I will," I said.

Julia waved, and I didn't know what to do with the unlit cigarette, so I slipped it into the pocket of my khaki pants where it broke in half and spilled out tiny tobacco leaves that I would fall asleep smelling that night.

The next day was Saturday, and I checked in with Mr. Solece. A friend was sleeping in a chair next to this bed, and I wanted to tell the man that he could go home and rest and come back later, because I knew that Mr. Solece was still not ready to go, but I knew my mother would not allow me to say such thing, not to a guest, not to anyone. So I brought the man a cup of tea and slice of fresh baked bread from the kitchen instead, and Mr. Solece woke up and wanted a slice of bread too.

"With honey," he said. "And cinnamon."

And he ate it happily when I brought it back to his room.

When I got to Julia and Oscar's room, I saw that she was quietly rocking Oscar near the window watching the waves crash on black rocks below.

"I've never slept next to the ocean," she said when I came into her room. "It gave me good dreams—I dreamt Oscar was smiling at me. That everything was good. That he was all better. You know, cured."

She rocked back and forth and I could smell her tears before they fell.

"I've had dreams like that about my dad," I said moving closer to her. "I lost him when I was little and sometimes I wake up and think he is still alive, that he never left."

Julia turned and looked at me.

"Do you want to hold him?"

"Sure," I said and she stood up and set Oscar carefully in my arms. He was warm and soft in my arms and smelled like the flower of a clover. I slid my finger into his tiny hand, but he did not grasp hold.

"He likes to be rocked," Julia said, so I took her place in the chair.

"What happened to your hair?" she said standing behind me, touching the matted pieces of hair.

"Gum," I said. "I have an appointment at ten. They are going to have to chop it all off."

"That is a nasty," Julia said holding the clump of hair in her hand. "If you want me to, I think I can get it out. I had a foster mom who used ice to get gum out of my hair once."

"Really," I said and directed her to the kitchen and told her that they would give her anything she needed back there and to bring us back some chocolate chip cookies, because they were always making cookies in the afternoon. My mother believed that food could be healing and made sure that there was comfort food for not only the patients, but for the patient's family and friends.

Julia left and came back with a bowl of ice and a plate of warm cookies and two coffees.

"Now let's see what I can do," Julia said as she held ice onto the gum.

I tiny trickle of cold water ran down my neck and Julia wiped it quickly away with her sleeve.

"They didn't think he'd live for more than a few hours," Julia said and I knew she was looking at Oscar in my arms, "but he kept on breathing into the next day, and I told them that they had to feed him, that I didn't want my baby to be hungry, so they hooked him up to this tube, she says pointing to where it ran into his nose, and he's been with me for a five days."

Julia walked around the chair and bent over Oscar and kissed him on the cheek.

"He's sweet," I said. "He really is."

She went back to working on my hair. She was gentle and patient and never tugged or pulled.

"There," she said when she was finished. "Look at that!"

My hair was combed clean—the gum broken into tiny frozen pieces and gone.

Julia took Oscar from me and laid him down on the bed.

"Thank you," I said and ran my fingers through the back of my hair. I wanted to hold him again. I wanted to feel his tiny body in the crook of my arm.

"Do you want to see if we can take Oscar for a walk down to the beach?" I said. I wanted to be outside with Oscar and Julia. The didn't belong in this place.

"You'd like that, wouldn't you?" Julia said to Oscar. "You'd like to see the ocean."

My mother agreed that the ocean air would sooth Oscar's lungs, that it would comfort him, so I grabbed my hat and sunscreen while Julia wrapped Oscar up in a blanket and we placed him in a stroller that a nurse had found for Julia and took him down a tarred path that led to the beach.

We sat in the warm sand and watched the waves crash against the shore.

"I want him to touch the ocean," Julia said and carefully unwrapped Oscar's tiny feet from his blanket and walked him down to the water. I slipped off my shoes and followed them.

We waited for a wave to recede and then when it did, Julia dipped his feet into the water and then wrapped him back up and carried him back to our blanket in the sand.

We spent the rest of that weekend together. I showed Julia and Oscar around the gardens, introduced them to

Mr. Solece who was in the room across the hall, sitting up in his bed.

"Beautiful, beautiful boy," Mr. Solece sang to Oscar and then turned to Julia, "Leonard and I always wanted a child. We wanted a family, but couldn't, so we ended up with four spoiled grey hounds instead."

Mr. Solece held Oscar's hand, and I could see that touching the tiny hand seemed to make Mr. Solece even stronger. He sat up straighter. He smiled. His skin took on a warm glow.

After school, one day, I took Julia and Oscar to a place where orange and pink and purple starfish clung to black rocks. Julia had never seen a live starfish before, and I held Oscar as she waded into the tide pool to touch their hard bumpy skin.

"They are so strong," she said when she came back to us.

We watched the tide rise. We watched the powerful waves pound against the rocks where the starfish clung. Not one of them fell off, not one of them let go.

"Hold on like the starfish," I whispered to Oscar. "Hold on. Don't go."

And Oscar lived through the week, and so did all my mother's other patients. No one died.

"He's growing," Julia said looking at Oscar in her arms one day. "He's getting bigger."

"I know," I said. "He's growing bigger every day."

And every day I fell more and more in love with Oscar. He and Julia became my family. We were happy even though Oscar was dying.

By the following Sunday, the hospice no longer felt like a place of death. It was louder than it had been for years. Patients were laughing and talking with visitors in their rooms. All the dying were living. They wanted to go outside in the sun, to be wheeled around the garden and down to the beach. They wanted to eat ice cream and cookies and freshly baked bread.

The kitchen worked nonstop and House of Peace began to smell like a bakery—cinnamon and melted butter and chocolate chip cookies.

Everyone was in a holding pattern. No one left. And the waiting list for a room at House of Peace grew longer each day.

"I've never seen so many not moving onto the next stage," my mother said to me when I found her in her office late one night. She looked tired. The living were wearing her out more than the dying ever had.

"What if the doctors were wrong about Oscar," I said. "He's growing."

My mother shook her head. "It is only a matter of time."

"How do you know?" I said. "How do you know that there isn't a chance? That maybe he could live a year or maybe two or three."

"His kidneys are beginning to shut down," my mother said.

"Can't you do something," I said. "Can't you stop it. Can't you help him to live?"

She looked down at the blue file on her desk.

"This has become too much for you," my mother said finally standing up from behind her desk and sitting in a chair next to mine. "I should've never asked you to be a part of this."

"No," I said. "I'm fine. I like it here."

"I think next week, when school is out, you get away from here for a while. This is not healthy. I see that now. I see what I have done to you."

"I won't go if Julia and Oscar are still here," I said.

"They will be gone," she said slowly and quietly. "I'm sorry, but they will be gone by then."

But I didn't believe her. The scent of death had disappeared that week and it seemed as if it would never return.

Another week passed, and each day after school I went to straight to Julia and Oscar's room. One day I took them up to our apartment and we sat together on my bed.

"Do you ever wish that your house stayed the same. That you didn't have so many sick people downstairs."

"No," I said. "The house was too big, too empty for just the two of us. I remember how I kept losing my mom. Calling to her and calling to her and finally finding her crying in her room. It was good that she did this. And I'm glad, but not glad that you and Oscar are here."

And I didn't want the two of them to leave my room. I wanted them to stay with me. I wanted them to live upstairs, not downstairs, but my mother said they couldn't stay in our apartment, that it wasn't right for me to have brought them up there, so that night, I snuck out and slept with Julia and Oscar in their room downstairs.

The next morning, the three of us sat by the window and watched a storm roll in across the ocean. The wind created tiny sand-cyclones down on the beach.

"We should read to Oscar," I said. I had brought some old books that I used to love—books that my father used to read to me. "He should hear some of these."

"I don't think he can hear," Julia said and handed Oscar to me. She looked sad and tired.

"He'll feel the story then. He'll feel the vibrations of our words."

"Why don't you read to him. I'm going to go out for a smoke," Julia said taking a lighter off the dresser in the room and disappearing down the hall.

So I read to Oscar from my favorite books: *Make Way for Ducklings* and *Green Eggs and Ham*, *Scruffy the Tugboat* and *Paddington Bear*.

I felt as if Oscar was listening.

Good-bye day, good evening moon. Why do you always appear so soon?

And it was then that I smelled the sweet smell, the sweetest scent I'd ever smelled. I looked out the window and watched the ocean's waves curl and unwind in great rolls.

"Julia," I said when I smelled the lingering remains of cigarette smoke from behind me. "Oscar is leaving us."

"Now?"

I nodded my head.

"How do you know?"

I didn't say anything, but I thought that maybe, being his mother, she could smell it too.

"Hold him," I said handing him to her. "Put your face to his. Do you smell that sweet scent?"

"Yes," she said

"Like the smell of an orange soda? Like an Orange Crush?"

This made Julia laugh and then she started to cry. "What does it mean?"

And I thought maybe that we could keep his life from escaping, keep him with us if we wrapped him up in a blanket, kept his life from leaving him.

"Hold him in your arms. Hold him tightly to your chest," I said and I wrapped them both up in a blanket on the bed and lay next to them, my arm across them both, but the sweet scent continued to fill the room, it grew stronger and stronger.

"You are loved, you are loved, you are loved," I whispered in Oscar's ears as Julia wept.

They wrapped Oscar up in a beautiful white patchwork quilt that Edith had made for him, and Julia carried him to the hearse that was waiting outside. The driver gently took him from Julia's arms and we watched the black car disappear down the drive.

Julia could barely stand. She hadn't eaten. She hadn't even had a sip of water.

"I'm sorry," I said and brought her up to our apartment and had her lay down in my bed, because I couldn't bring her back to the room where she and Oscar had been.

I kissed her on her forehead and told her I'd be back with some food, and went downstairs to find my mother instead.

"Julia needs to stay with us," I said when I found my mother in her office. "We can't just send her away."

"Her social worker will be her soon. He has already made arrangements for her to go to a new foster home."

"No," I said. "We are the only ones who know. Who understand. We held Oscar. I loved him."

"I'm sorry," my mother said.

"Can't she stay with us? Can't she just live here? With us?"

"Avery," my mother said, "I'm sorry, but she can't. My job was to take care of Oscar and now he has passed."

A nurse knocked on the doorway to tell my mother that another patient was passing.

"Mr. Solece?" I said.

"Yes," the nurse said.

The holding pattern was over.

"I have go. I have patients to attend to," my mother said.

"What about the living?" I said.

"I'm sorry," my mother said. "You need get away from all this. You need to be with the living."

"Julia is living. Julia is here."

"Other arrangements have been made. She will be taken care of and we will attend Oscar's funeral and you can keep in touch with her."

"Let her stay," I said again. "Let this be her home."

"I can't," my mother said. "I can't."

As the sun slowly sunk behind clouds on the horizon, Julia and I sat in the garden waiting for her social worker to arrive.

She held a cigarette in her hand and I watched as she inhaled the smoke and held it in her lungs, then slowly released it, a gray tail sliding from her lips.

"I thought they might be wrong about Oscar," she said. "I thought that he would live."

"So did I," I said. "I really did."

Julia leaned against me and passed me the cigarette.

"We were happy here," she said.

I inhaled the smoke. It burned my eyes, my lungs, my nose, and I could smell nothing after she was gone.

"Orange Crush" originally appeared in *Water~Stone Review*.

Born From Red

by Stephanie Hutton

The school is on lock-down for a random colour check and I hear whispers that Leila has climbed out of the bathroom window, taking her painted toenails to safety. The rule is absolute; we must not see red. We line up in rows of cream and grey with our shirt sleeves rolled up. Our skirts touch our knees, showing pimply flesh where the hairs have been waxed as we are not permitted blades. Any scratch or cut must be covered with a bandage. It is safer to stay at home until your body is back the way it is intended—without the colour of the devil.

I heard there is a nurse who checks that all girls are taking their medication—no menstruation is allowed of course, as that is the fiercest red there is. There was a girl in the year above me who vomited out her meds, or forgot them, or had a dark desire to see her own blood. She was dismissed that day. We had to hang our heads and stare at the floor as she was escorted out. I wriggled my toes to wave goodbye but the rigid leather of my shoes hid my cowardly act.

After the checks, there is shared relief that shows itself in skittishness and rumours. It is the one afternoon of the term when the male instructors lean back in their chairs and permit whispers between us. I wonder at their intentions. The best way to keep control is to let our mouths spread stories and blame. My classmates' tongues click away at her name—Leila, Leila, Leila. I sit straight-backed and count with each breath to tame my heartbeats. Even as I recite poetry in my head, I see the image of my blood-red heart beating her name, sending the urge to run down into my legs. I am grateful that it is Friday and I have two days of freedom to find her. She will not return to class on Monday.

Once the sun is high up above us, I tell dad I have botany specimens to collect and will be back by supper time. He is gluing small parts onto a ship that looks no different to any of the others he has made. He glances up from his handiwork to me and—although I squeezed my hands into a fist in preparation—I can't help but look away from the scarlet filaments that streak his eyes. These rivulets of red tell a story of lonely nights with only a vodka bottle to hold. My mother chose not to move to the safety of this village before I even started school. We do not speak of her. I hear the pulsing blood in my ears that keeps me alive while threatening to ruin me.

"No sharps, stay clean Anna," he says and wraps some bread in cloth for me to take. I hold my breath as I kiss the top of his head, as if to stop him inhaling my intentions.

I take the path that leads from the back of our row of cottages towards the woods. The bluebells that kissed these grounds have already gone for another year. I walk fast enough to ache the back of my legs and burn my chest. Stillness or speed, nothing in-between. The curves of the path are as familiar as those of my signature. I once tried to walk the length with my eyes closed, certain that I could navigate the route. The elation of the first twenty yards was smashed as I tripped over and landed on my hands. Criss-cross lines in the forbidden colour kept me off school for a week and caused me such shame I stayed in bed with the drapes drawn to dull the hue.

I settle by the stream on a welcoming bank of grass to wait for her. This is our spot. She showed me how to fish with just a stick and fast hands. Leila wears no sun cream or hat so her skin is older than her years, brown and rich. I am slathered in lotion to ensure that no patches of red appear on my shoulder blades or across my nose. We are taught that lips are naturally pink, but Leila's are as red as they are plump. She laughed when I told her this, curling my hair behind my ear. She told me of food from her grandmother's farm hidden high in the hills. The luscious tomatoes and sweet dripping apples, the opposite of green.

I doze in the warmth, the sunlight drifting through the mesh of my hat.

Leila speaks my name and tickles the back of my hand with a fern. My words won't come. She flings off her shoes and wobbles on one foot to show me her toenails. The rumours were true—they are painted a red so shiny I squint.

"I've got something for us to try, if you like." Leila talks through her hands, which curl around each word and continue talking after her mouth stops. Sometimes they talk instead of her lips, like the time she pulled me to the roadside to look at the crushed bloodied carcass of a deer. She uncurls her hand and shows me little red and white mushrooms. I clench my teeth. Then nod.

We climb a little further into the trees for cover. Leila doesn't get out of breath like I do. She knows facts that are not in any book that we are allowed. I don't ask her how she knows. She tells me that these are toadstools, like in the fairy tales. I recall them being dusky pink and pure white. Leila laughs with her head tipped back, the length of her neck on view.

"Listen Anna, you don't have to take them with me. They could make us pretty sick. But before they do, they will show us a different world." She is glowing. I tell myself that my nausea is excitement. My last weekend with Leila. I catch myself digging my nails into my palms and stop before any marks are made.

Leila arranges the toadstools on a piece of bark and chops them with a knife she pulls from her pocket. I long to run my finger along its edge. We chew the foamy pieces and sip river water from a flask, then we share my bread. Leila tells me she is going to go and work on her grandmother's farm, just outside the limits of the village. They keep animals I have never been near. My head starts to whirl as she tells me about lambs getting stuck in their mothers and pigs that reject their young. She has not just learnt this from letters sneaked in through the delivery boy—she must have been out there, in the world we were born into. The elbow I'm leaning on collapses under me, so I lie flat on the grass hearing the thud of the land. Leila's legs shake until she drops down to the ground near me and lies down. I feel the sting of bile at the back of my throat.

"Don't fight it Anna, let it show you things. I'm right here."

She grabs my hand and the trees bend towards me as if to hold us together. I can't tell if it is the trees spinning around and around or us. Or have we only just noticed that the world is turning? The grass underneath my body shoots up around us and springs into flowers larger than my head. Ripples run up and down my body as if I am lying on the riverbed.

I float up above the forest floor, higher and higher. Our village of green fields, pink flowers and white houses. There is the school, glowing so brightly I squeeze my eyes for protection. Then I dive down, down towards the ground, which opens beneath me. I land in a labyrinth of tunnels and press my back against hot earthy walls. Rivers of red run under the school, flowing outwards to escape to the forest. Swimming in the claret waters are beautiful women with their swollen pregnant forms. They turn to float on their backs, smiling and singing to their unborn. Standing waist-high in the lapping water, a couple intertwine while kissing—their hands grip and swirl across each other. I look more closely at the liquid. In the place of disgust, I feel peace and passion and what it is to be a woman. We were all born from red.

My body rises and floats easily out of the tunnels as my eyes linger on the scene I wish to stay in. Everything turns pure white as I return to my breathing body. The lulling waves change to stormy seas and I turn to my side to retch again and again. Sweat pours from the back of my neck as I free my stomach of all its bitterness.

My limbs start to obey my commands. The trees are back in their place, nothing but tall conifers swaying in the wind, oblivious to us. I turn to Leila and smile. She squeezes my hand in hers. Then I remember. My mother's hand encasing mine as she sang sweet melodies. My father screaming that her summer dress showed her off like a whore. The smash of his bottle. Red flowing down her arm. A pool of blood with shards of glass between us. Her shouting at me to keep away, to go to my room and stay under the covers. And later, again and again, dad on his knees, rocking forward and back as he prayed. Mumbling words through liquor-warmed lips, begging the Lord to keep us safe from the devil that lives in all women.

The danger is not out there, beyond the pastel safety of our village limits. It is not inside me. It is not a colour. I stand up and scan the higher land beyond the fencing. Paths curve their way up through the sloping fields—

invitations in a thousand directions. One of them leads to my mother.

Leila still holds my hand as we make our way along an overgrown path towards the outskirts of the village. Our embracing fingers do the work of words. As the sun sets, the pink and white of the sky merge at the horizon into a deep red.

"Born From Red" originally appeared in *Bristol Short Story Prize Anthology Volume 10*.

The Meantime

by Zoë Johnson

6

The first time it happens, you're small. Too small to recognize him, anyway. You are six and he is … well. Everyone above your cousin's age tends to melt together at the edges into a grainy fog of "older." So you're not entirely sure.

You'll learn later that he was twenty-seven. It's a fact that matters very little to you at the time, but very much to you later on.

The cheap foam of your small flip-flops wasn't made for this kind of frantic childhood running on hot summer pavement. They tug at the space between your toes. Your heels slip off the sides, slapping sharply against the sidewalk as you run.

Roxy and her orange-striped tail flicker out of sight as she rounds the corner ahead. Judging by the running and the hissing, she hadn't enjoyed you tugging on it as much as you had.

You round the corner after her and there Roxy is, weaving figure eights around the turned up cuffs of his jeans over worn boots.

He's squatted down, reaching out his hand out to her, but straightens up as you slow to a trot.

"Is this your cat?" he asks as you reach him. You have to shade your eyes and squint to look up at him, the sun glaring and painful in the afternoon sky just behind his shoulders.

"Her name's Roxy," you reply. Your hair is long at six years old and you brush it clumsily from your eyes. "She was running away."

He bends down to scoop the cat into his arms, and for a moment you are shocked into stillness, amazed that she allows it.

He crouches down in front of you once more with Roxy secure in his arms, smile gentle and framed by the barest hint of stubble. For a moment, he reminds you of your father. It's something about the smile and the nose, maybe. Not the eyes, though. They're the kind of hazel that your mother has. That you have.

He cradles Roxy so very gently and you are momentarily transfixed by his hands.

"You should be nicer to her," he says, ducking his chin down at Roxy in gesture. She's begun purring softly.

"I *am* nice to her," you pout, crossing your arms. "She just doesn't like me."

He laughs. You reach out and press your hand down along Roxy's back.

"Ah—! Ah, easy there, kiddo," he interrupts, jerking Roxy away from you. "Be gentle." Then, softer. "She likes gentle."

"Seems like she just likes *you.*" You scowl at him and at Roxy, down at the weeds clawing their way through the cracks in the sidewalk.

A tight coil of jealousy blooms quickly and easily inside of your small chest and later you will begin to suspect that it never truly left you.

Your words make him laugh, although you didn't think anything you said was that funny. His is a laugh that seems to climb up through him to reach his mouth and he tips his head back with the force of it. Roxy's ears prick up, eyes wide at the sudden shaking of his chest.

"She'll like you too. Just give it time," he manages after a moment, voice still bright with residual laughter. "And like I said, be *gentle* with her."

Leaning toward you, he gestures down with a jerk of his chin and you practice being gentle with Roxy while he cradles her in his arms, purring and warm.

"What's your name?" you ask eventually. You don't think you've ever managed to pet Roxy for this long without getting scratched.

"Charlie," he answers.

Your hand stills on Roxy's back and you tilt your head, considering.

"I like that name," you declare. "It's a lot better than mine." You wrinkle your nose and spit the word "Angela" with distaste. He licks his lips, considering; you notice they're badly chapped.

"You know what? I agree with you," he says softly. "Angela doesn't suit you very well, does it?"

You shake your head. "Uh-uh. I wish Charlie was my name instead," you say.

He looks down at Roxy, her eyes nearly closed in contentment. He smiles again but this time doesn't reply.

10

You don't see him again until you're ten. He's younger this time around. But then again, this time around you're also older. Old enough to start asking him the right sorts of questions.

At ten, your hair is still long and your parents still call you Angela.

He's in his late teens, leaning against the metal frame of the swing set in his khaki shorts and Converse sneakers. You're pumping your legs back and forth, trying to gain momentum as the metal creaks dangerously with the motion.

"How does it work?" you ask him.

"The Visiting thing?" He lets out a long breath and shakes his head, arms crossed over his chest. His eyes follow the back and forth of the swing. "I'm really not sure. It just sort of … happens? I get this dizziness—like the ground is tilting away from me. Then the world slides sideways, sort of. And then I'm—" He stops, swallowing, gaze falling to the wood chips blanketing the ground. "Uh, some other time. For us. You know?"

He shrugs, like he knows as well as you do that the explanation didn't actually explain much. And, well, that's just it. He *should* know as well as you do.

But the thing is, you *don't* know. You don't get why he is *him* like this; why you are *you* like you are now. How the two of you are supposed to be two ticks on the same timeline, and yet there is such a dissonance between you two.

"I haven't been able to figure out when it'll happen. It just kinda comes on. And I never know how long I'll be Visiting each time. Or how old you—I—we'll—" He lets out a frustrated breath, smooths a hand over the top of his head, tugs the short ponytail of his dark hair tighter. "Whatever."

You don't say anything, focusing on the movement of your legs, on reaching the highest you can go. Your stomach lurches at the backwards motion and you wonder if the Visiting he's talking about might feel a little like this.

The wind whips your long hair behind you, away from your body, and for a moment it almost feels as though you don't have it at all. The metal chains squeak horribly in your gripping fingers.

This time, when you reached the highest point, you launch yourself off the swing. For a moment you are weightless—suspended above the ground and the layer of wood chips.

Twisting your head around as you fall, you find yourself at his eye level a split-second before you hit the ground. It makes you wonder how long you will have to spend growing until you reach his height.

You land badly. Off balance, with one knee already under you taking most of your weight, the other twists out behind you, buckling on impact. You cry out at the twist in your stomach and force jolting heavy up the length of your arms when you slam your hands down to catch yourself.

You hear the crunch of wood chips underfoot as he jogs toward you where you are half crumpled on the ground, palms stinging, shorts dirt-smeared. He reaches out a hand to help you up. When you look up at him, the sun is in your eyes again.

He pulls you to your feet, a flash of sharp pain stabbing suddenly into your leg. Looking down, you see dirt and wood-dust smeared across your knee, blood oozing steadily down the length of your shin.

"Oh yeah, don't worry about that," he says, following your line of sight to the gash. He points to his own knee where the thin pink line of a faint scar wobbles along the bottom of his kneecap. "It heals up in a few days."

You study his long-healed scar tissue while your own knee sears with the icy needles of a fresh wound.

"You don't—" You stop. Consider. Squint up against the sun to study him. "You don't look like me, though."

"You don't exactly look like you, either," he replies.

And there, on the playground beside the swing set with blood dripping down your leg, it occurs to you that there might be so much more than you'd realized between where you are and where he is—between the Now of you and the Then of him.

And it sharpens from an abstract, the Then—becomes a solid shape emerging from fog into the sight of his scarred knee and short ponytail and masculinity lit from behind him by the brightness of the sun.

That night, after your parents have gone to sleep, you tiptoe down the dark hush of the hallway to the bathroom with a pair of your mother's sewing scissors hidden up your sleeve.

The slow *snip, snip* of the scissors sounds so loud in the otherwise silent house.

You don't stop cutting until your hair barely brushes the line of your jaw. Pulling it back into a ponytail at the base of your skull has loose hair shedding across your hands like falling pine needles. The lines of a million fissure cracks scored across your fledgling hands.

You look into the mirror and you smile.

12

By the time the world slides away from you for the first time, you go by Charlie.

You're twelve. And despite the nausea and the light-headedness that knocks you off your internal balance, it is a relief to feel the tilting spin of it. It's a reminder and a promise. It really did happen. ~~You~~ He *will* happen.

You find yourself in a bedroom—your bedroom, but also somehow *not* your bedroom—and he is sitting at the desk in flannel pajama pants and a Spiderman t-shirt. He looks up from the laptop open in front of him. The screen's glow cuts harsh blue angles from the contours of his face.

"Oh, hey," he says. He pauses and squints at you a little. "This was the first time, wasn't it?"

You nod, looking around the room instead of at him. He stays seated at the desk chair as you take uncertain, wandering steps. You can't help but examine the things on his shelves that are also on your shelves—can't help but wonder at the ones that have yet to become your treasured and sentimental belongings.

"Your voice..." you start, turning to face him, but you stop at the sight of the grin on his face.

"Doesn't it sound great?" he agrees. You swallow. It sounds low and boyish and *right*.

"So I guess we tell Mom and Dad at some point, huh?" The pitch of your speech grates even more sharply in such close proximity to his. The bed sinks differently beneath your weight when you go to sit, pulling your knees up and against your chest.

He nods. You wrap your arms around your legs, chin resting on your knees.

"When do I—" you stutter and stop. "When do we start hormones?"

There is his smile again, a smile like relief and pride and exultation. And it *hurts*, somehow, for reasons too large and tangled for your young clumsy fingers to attempt to unravel.

"Sophomore year. Been on T for about a year now. I've started getting some facial hair too. Wanna see?" He is glowing with it.

You're only twelve but the terror of a puberty that your mind does not belong is hurtling towards you. It looms and stretches large—an encroaching shadow that clutches at the edges of your child's form.

You are across the room standing at ~~your~~ his desk before you can think. Something tightens around the base of your throat.

That thing inside of your chest is still there, fermenting and souring every time you are reminded of what you must still wait to be. And there is a part of you that thinks perhaps your body is too tiny to hold such a complicated and toxic jealousy. Perhaps it might always be.

He tilts his chin up and away, angling the sharp line of his jaw towards you. His mouth is still stretched into that inevitable grin.

Doesn't he remember? You wonder at your own thoughtlessness. How could he just forget how much being here—you—Now—on *this* side of the things you need simply *eviscerates* you?

There is a distance between the two of you (the *two* of *you*) that you have yet to travel. There is a stretching route, an unassailable interval, and in this moment that you begin to understand the true scope of it—how much Waiting is left before you. And there is something so uniquely gutting about the visceral impossibility of shortening that gap, of traversing it more quickly.

You realize that your hand is shaking as you raise it toward the dark beginnings of stubble along the underside of his jaw.

Then you blink.

And you are standing alone back in your own darkened bedroom. Your hand is still outstretched, reaching towards empty air.

15

Water is streaming down from your eyelashes, the tile of the shower wall warping and scattering through the prism of the droplets in your eyes. His voice is hard to hear over the thundering hiss of the water and the hiccupping, shuddering sound of your breathing.

Here, curled in on yourself, spine curved inward like the pulled-taut arch of a bow, he feels so far away from you. Your knees are pulled up to your chest against the water-heavy fabric of your sports bra as if maybe, if you press yourself in hard enough, you can make it disappear for good.

"I hate it too," he tells you.

You don't know how old he is this time; you've been sitting beneath the shower spray since before he showed up. He is at least seventeen, you know, because of the lowness of his voice (*twomoreyears twomoreyears*). But besides that he is nothing but the blurry outline against the white of the shower curtain. An ephemeral shadow, a hazy possibility, the most visceral of torments.

It almost doesn't seem like he is there at all. Sometimes, during the journey across the deserts of the Waiting, you nearly convince yourself he isn't. Because it seems so unlikely, so distant—the destination of him.

"I ca—" you heave in a breath and your whole body rocks with the effort; you squeeze your eyes shut at how high and how *feminine* your sadness sounds. "I—I can't live like this. I can't do it."

"Yes you can," he replies. "You can survive this."

You shake your head, loose strands of hair sticking wetly to your cheeks. You squeeze your legs against your chest until it is hard to breathe. You try to focus on the hair plastered against your calves made darker with water, on how they make your legs look like other boys'—like they're supposed to.

You try to conjure up sounds of a waitress yesterday forming the words *sir* and *young man*. Try to cement the image of your English teacher smiling and nodding and easily shifting to *Charlie* and *him* and firm unwavering steel—*you will respect your fellow students in my classroom by using Charlie's correct name, Ms. Tanner*. Of jeans in the men's section dressing room that fit you well, of shirts that fall just right to make your chest look flat. Of your dad's slow and measured voice and *you're my child and I will love you even if I don't understand*.

You try to calculate if these sparse rations are enough to survive on for the next few years; scattered oases, handfuls of seconds grasped with frantic desperation.

You shouldn't have to *survive* years of your life. You shouldn't have to arrive starving and delirious from thirst at each and every scrap of respite.

You shouldn't have to live *through* pieces of your life, you think, and your chest aches with the magnitude of what lies before you, of what you are being told to *survive*. Through the constant, unending daily *shehermissma'am-younglady*. Through the skin-crawling nausea every time you take off your chest binder. Through the drive-by hallway hisses of *fucked up girl thinks she's a real boy*, of *tranny*, of *faggot*. Through the—Through the—

Fingers clutching at your hair, you are trembling with the enormity of it; there is so much inside of you, coiling and expanding beneath a chest that you cannot stand even long enough to take a *shower* and yet are being forced to *live beneath for **years**—*

He does not speak again. And you do not look over to where the outline of his form had haunted the shower curtain.

The water eventually runs cold and you stand on uncertain legs to shut it off. When you finally pull back the curtain, the bathroom is empty again.

17
"You're a freshman this year, right?"

"Mmm."

You pluck a pebble from the grass beside you and hurl it into the river that cuts through the middle of campus. He's resting his chin atop his folded arms and you both watch it soar, watch it plunk into the water, watch the ripples snatched away by the current's pull before they have a chance to spread outwards.

"That makes you seventeen this time, huh?"

"Mmm. College and all that. It's … better. It's better being away from home. People here only know me as Charlie. It's nice." You card your hand through the nearby grass, feeling for another rock. "What about you?"

"Twenty-three now." He pauses. "I've got a consultation scheduled for top surgery in about a month."

You swallow against the sudden tight feeling in your throat. In your chest.

"Well thank god for that," you manage but it comes out sounding as bitter as it feels. Twenty-three feels positively *eons* away.

"I need to stop doing that, huh?" he asks, eyes still on the water. He sighs and leans back on his hands, legs stretching out in front of him.

"Yeah," you agree. You huff and it's a disgusted, amused sort of noise. "It's really shitty."

"Have we always been so bad at talking to ourself?" he asks wryly.

He runs his hand over his hair to tighten his ponytail at the base of his skull. It's weird seeing the habit from the other side like this since you've started doing it.

One of your shoulders scrunches up in the suggestion of a shrug and you chuck another rock towards the river.

He doesn't speak for a while. You just continue sitting in the grass, physics textbook abandoned beside you, tossing rocks toward the river.

"Time is a weird thing for us, isn't it?" he finally says.

"Time is weird for everybody. Get off your high horse, old man."

He laughs.

"Hey, so…" You trail off, tongue darting out to wet your chapped lips. He lets you think, silently watches the water and the ducks raucously making their way downstream. "When does Mom come around?"

You *hate* how small your voice sounds when you say it. You've been on testosterone for years but it's always when you're sad and scared and uncertain that the wobble of your voice carries with it those old patterns, the ones that scream *girl* and *female*, and you are burying your hands in the grass, clutching until your knuckles are white.

"She … Well, she…" The hesitation in his voice tells you everything.

"Yeah, ok." You sound choked. You blink quickly against the pricking of hot tears because, goddammit, no one will believe you're a boy if you *cry* in *public*. Jesus fucking Christ. "Whatever."

Twenty-three. *Twenty-three* and your mother still hasn't—

"Dad's trying his best. Says we have to be patient with h—" he starts to say but you cut him off, shaking your head, the movement jerky and badly restrained.

"*Please* don't," you manage, head tucked down low against your chest, eyes squeezed shut so tightly it hurts. You've never been able to break the habit of curling yourself into a ball like this. "Not you too. I can take all that *just be patient, it gets better* shit from everyone else but not from you too. Not when you should *know* what—"

You break off because your voice is perilously close to cracking. It is through sheer force of will you are keeping back tears. Bringing your hands up from the grass, you dig the heels of your palms into your eyes until they force bursts of bright yellow spots across the backs of your eyelids.

"I'm sorry," he mutters beside you. Beyond you the ducks call loudly to each other and the river hisses. Underneath it all you can hear his slow breathing whistling through his nose. You wonder if he may be recovering from a cold.

You close your eyes and you breathe.

"Yeah, well," you swallow hard, trying to get your voice to settle. "Sorry doesn't make it easier for me to get out of bed tomorrow."

You pull your knees up and rest your forehead against them.

"I know that."

"Then don't fucking say that shit to me anymore," you mutter down at your thighs. "It *hurts*, okay?"

And the words sound so hollow, so pathetic, that you hate yourself for their fragility for a moment.

You are a series of asymptotes. The directions and angles and lengths of the lines flicker into new configurations second after second yet remain continuously and infinitely unable to intersect.

He doesn't say anything for a long while and you wonder if maybe he's gone, that the Visiting has decided to yank him back to wherever he's from, where he is past so much of what you still have to live through. You don't know because you can't bring yourself to lift your head from your knees.

"Why can't we stop hurting ourself?" you ask quietly. You feel twelve again. Ten again. Six again. Back at the beginning of things. "I'm just so tired of hurting."

Perhaps this is to be your existence—to be a stupidly narrow-sighted dog, always chasing, snapping at its own tail in winding looping circles of time.

When you finally lift your head, the grass is bright and he is gone and you are alone again.

23

When he shows up in your apartment, he staggers sideways, a rookie sailor trying to balance on a ship only he can feel rocking.

You dart forward to steady him, grabbing at his forearm, his shoulder.

From up this close, he looks almost sickly. His eyes are too bright, skin shining with a light sheen of sweat. His lips are chapped and there are dark circles under his eyes.

The look of him tells you he's twenty. You remember being twenty.

"Thanks," he mutters and yanks himself out of your grasp the moment he's steadied himself.

"Sure," you reply, stuffing your suddenly empty hands into your pockets.

His posture is slumped, hunched in on himself, and his gaze darts about the room warily. He tilts his head in a vague gesture at his surroundings.

"You live here now?" he asks. "By yourself?"

"For a few months now, yeah."

"Hmm." He nods, his eyes cataloguing the living room with cautious, analytical sweeps.

It's quiet then. He is, and you are. And you'd nearly forgotten how quiet those few years had made you. How hackled. How distrustful. Of your parents and your friends and your doctors and your lovers. Of everyone and everything. Even of yourself on the bad days. You don't know why you can't remember if this Visit happened on one of those bad days.

You lick your lips, slide an awkward hand over the top of your head.

"I, uh … Lemme go get you something to drink. Or eat. I dunno if you're hungry." You turn to head into the kitchen, but you're halted by the cobra strike motion of his hand snagging in the material of your hoodie sleeve.

"How do—" The words seem to eek out of him, the frantic burst of steam from a pipe's pinprick rupture—something that high pressure forces out through the smallest of openings.

The sound of it has you turning back to him, his shoulders hunched, his face tilted down towards the floor. And with his arm outstretched like this he looks so very young to you now.

You think he might hate you for that if you said it aloud.

He still isn't looking at you as he takes a deep breath, squeezes his eyes shut.

"How…" He starts. Stops. Licks his lips. Breathes. "How do you deal with the … the loneliness of it?"

It's a moment before you are able to speak. Because you are not hurting as much anymore, here in the now of it. But you are still hurting. Or maybe it's just that you hurt in different ways now.

You are a ship unmoored. Simultaneously, you are its anchor.

It's a painful puzzle, this untangling of old wounds from healing wounds from new wounds. It renders you an echoing labyrinth in this moment, an accordion stretch of mirrors reflecting onto one another into infinity. These things are yours and also not yours and somehow also something in between the two.

"I … don't really," you finally manage. "But seeing you helps. Reminds me … that I'm not wrong. Or broken, or whatever. It's hard to remember that sometimes."

He nods and he's still not looking at you. God, you were so small then.

This must be what it's like for an electron, you think distantly—to exist in a quantum state.

"I hate it. How things are for me. Us." His voice is quiet and tight like he's trying not to let it shake. "And it—It wouldn't even bother me so much, the things people say, if it just wasn't—If it wasn't—" Breaking off, he huffs out a frustrated breath and runs his hand along his pulled back hair.

"Everyday. All day," you supply, voice barely above a murmur. He nods, swallowing thickly.

"From almost everyone," he continues. "Even if they aren't doing it on purpose, it just—it just *shreds* me, you know? Being called *she* all the time. Being called crazy. A confused lesbian. An *abomination*. I just—" He looks so desperate, his eyes wide and bright and darting around the room like he might find something to grasp on to—a drowning swimmer clutching for purchase. "I know who I am and I just want to live my fucking life! That's all I want! That's *all I want!*"

You put your hands on his shoulders because you don't know how to do anything else.

"I understand," you tell him. "It sucks," you tell him. "You—We—Everyone like us deserves so much better," you tell him.

And before you can understand what's happening, his arms are around your waist and his face is pressed against your sternum. His breath is uneven and he smells like that macho deodorant you used to wear because it was 'manly guy' deodorant, because it ~~was~~ is hard to remember that you don't have to be other peoples' ideas of a man to be a man.

"I don't wanna go. Not yet, just—" His voice is very soft where it's muffled against your hoodie. You think you can feel him shaking. "Just a little longer, please."

You return your hand to his shoulder, sliding it down to his bicep. You look up at the ceiling and think again how much ~~you~~ he deserves better.

"I don't wanna be alone again. Not yet. Pleas—"

Before he can finish the word, your arms are empty. And you are left standing there with the soft, living heat of him slowly leaching itself from the fabric of your clothing.

25

You are twenty-five and you almost think you are imagining it when you spot him, a splotch of dark clothes and dark hair against the bright heat of late afternoon summer sun, standing there at the edge of the dock.

You swim in from the middle of the lake and heave yourself up the ladder, your loose hair dripping into your eyes. He doesn't move as you make your way to him; he just stands there and watches you, hands stuffed into the pockets of his jeans, saying nothing.

He wordlessly studies you with his jaw set, his brow creased, his eyes hard and yearning and fixed on the sight of your bare chest.

You stand, the air raising goosebumps along your soaking skin, and you let him look. You let him look at the scars, at your pectorals, at your face, then back again. You let him look—desperate and then venomous—then young and fragile—then back again.

And when he takes that step forward to close the distance, hand reaching towards the bared center of you, you let him do that too.

Your soaked swim trunks are dripping itchy rivulets down your calves, but you try your best to stay motionless when he finally touches you. His fingers are surprisingly warm against your still-drying skin.

Before you know it, both his hands are raised to your chest and his fingertips are mapping an outward sweep from the middle of your sternum, smoothing down feathers on a pair of misplaced wings.

"What's it like?" he asks finally and it startles you a little. His voice is thick. Rough. He stills his wandering touch, placing both palms flat against your chest in twin points of warmth.

"Exactly what you think it's going to be like," you answer after a moment. And you know how much the words hurt to hear. You hate that you said them anyway.

He doesn't speak again. Only squeezes his eyes shut tightly.

One of his hands drops, falling to hang beside his leg where his fingers curl inward, clenching into a fist. And you watch the motion as if you are watching five small and fragile versions of yourself curling in over themselves with a physical sort of grief.

He takes a deep and unsteady breath through his nose. Swallows thickly. Clenches his jaw.

He's trying not to cry, you realize. Still young and uncertain, he cannot block out the world when it says that in order for *him* to be a boy he has to be more boy than most.

You want to tell him that he is allowed to cry. That here, if nowhere else, the humanity of his tears will not be misgendered. You want to tell him that you cried when you were him. That you're going to. That somewhere in the sideways tilt of time, you might always be crying.

That somewhere in the sideways tilt of time, you are also happy.

You are a Schrodinger's paradox of a boy—a quantum particle of the most intensely human kind.

Managing not to pull him to you is a very near thing. You want to so desperately—to hug him to you, tell him that you have lived through this, that *he* will live through this. That things will be all right.

But you don't. This time, you manage not to.

Because you have learned that offering these kinds of empty platitudes from the other side of the Waiting is the kind of thing that only seems like the right thing when you aren't stuck in its midst. You have learned that from the After, "you will live through this" always has a way of reaching the Before sounding like "you still have all of it left to live through."

And you are just so tired of hurting yourself; the rest of the world ignores and hurts and hates you plenty without you doing it for them.

He just shakes his head, his eyes still screwed shut against the brightness of the sun.

"I know," you say. "I'm sorry," you say.

He doesn't speak. Just drops his other hand away from your skin. And he is gone.

27

It feels like a long, long time before the world slides away from you to reveal the baking cement of a sidewalk. The sun is high and sweltering, beating down on your shoulders from behind. And you are alone.

There is a flicker of orange as a small cat trots around the corner ahead. And the sight gives you the strange sensation of having lived this moment only moments before. Of having lived centuries since then.

You smile and bend down, beckoning with your hand outstretched. Because since you were here last you have been learning—for seconds, eons, lifetimes, maybe will always be learning—how to be gentle with the small fragile things running towards you.

Pocket Full of Posies

by Miriam Karmel

There's a finger bone from the hand of St. Teresa of Avila in a church in Spain. The saint's rosary beads are also on display, as is the cord she used to flagellate herself.

Ruth, the checker at Jewel Foods, saw the bone on her church group tour of Spanish cathedrals. While I was getting my money out, Ruth retrieved a picture postcard from beneath the register to show me what she'd seen. She's always been chatty. Lately, though, I sense she's been trying to entertain me, take my mind off things. I'm sorry I told her about my mother. My job. Still, Ruth's stories amuse me and I like her for calling a bone a bone.

At dinner, I told Hugh about St. Teresa. "That can be anyone's bone," I said. "Anyone's beads. Cord."

"Why would they make that up?" he said.

"Because they can? They made up an entire religion. Why not invent the props to go with it?"

Hugh said it would be bad luck to fake the relics of a saint. That was odd, coming from Mr. Precise. He's a calculator of carbon footprints. His job is to determine the amount of energy one uses by say, flying from Chicago to Paris. Then he finds ways to offset such profligate consumption. Suddenly, he's Mr. Superstitious. He'll say anything to contradict me.

*

First my mother died. Then I lost my job. Then while I was peeling butternut squash a man on the radio said, "Cooking is over." I shouted, "Look at me, wise guy! I'm cooking soup." Then the peeler slipped and gashed my finger. I trailed blood all the way across the kitchen floor to the bandage drawer.

At dinner, over squash soup, I told Hugh, "I'm thinking of going to Paris."

"As in France?"

"No," I said. "As in Paris, Georgia."

There is such a place. I found it in a book, *I Bet You Didn't Know*. There are twenty-six cities in the United States named Paris. There's a Paris, Ohio, a Paris, Kentucky, and a Paris, Missouri.

I've been reading books like *I Bet You Didn't Know*, hoping to discover what people do with their loved ones' ashes. At this point, I could write the book. I'd include the story about a woman in Connecticut who wears her son's ashes in a locket around her neck. And I'd mention the man who tossed a spoonful of his wife's ashes into the bouillabaisse he served at a luncheon following her memorial service. I bet you didn't know that!

What I don't know is what to do with my mother's ashes. I told Hugh I wished she'd been buried like my father, who is laid to rest in a plain pine box at the Jewish cemetery on the city's north side. He was lowered into the ground according to tradition, within twenty-four hours of breathing his last breath. It happened so fast my brother Barnet, who was on a Princess cruise to the Bahamas with his latest girlfriend, couldn't get back in time for the funeral. "There's something to be said for tradition," I told Hugh.

Hugh said, "You've got to do something with her, Vera. It isn't right." He thinks it's time to scatter my mother's ashes. He says she's *languishing*.

I reminded him about St. Teresa. "If a church in Spain can display her finger bone all these years, why can't I leave my mother on the mantle?"

"Your mother wasn't a saint," he said, and I said, "You never liked her." Then we fought.

*

She arrived by UPS one morning in May, though I didn't know it was her. The package sat on the front hall table for nearly a week awaiting Hugh's return from a conference. Hugh is always ordering something—a widget for his bicycle, worms for his composter, an out-of-print book. I set the package in the pile with the rest of his mail.

"This must be yours," Hugh said. I was washing lettuce for dinner and he was at the kitchen table going through the mail. He held up a small container. He turned it over;

148

shook it. He even pressed it to his ear, as if he were listening for the ocean in a seashell.

"Mine?" I turned off the water, wiped my hands on my jeans and took it from him. It was a tin box imprinted with a pretty floral motif. I said it looked like it might contain an assortment of English toffee. "But who would be sending us candy, of all things?"

Then Hugh read aloud from a note that was in the packing box. Before he finished, I tried handing the tin back, as if we were kids playing Hot Potato. Quickly, he stepped away, picked up a penknife and sliced through an envelope. I sank into a chair and cradled the tin. "I didn't expect her to arrive by UPS," I said.

*

I was staring at the kitchen floor when Barnet called. The dog had just tracked in mud. Hugh had tracked in something he'd picked up on his running shoes. I was thinking I'd have to get out the mop and bucket and ammonia. I'd have to run the water until it was hot, and while it was running I'd think about Hugh carping if I let the water run while brushing my teeth. I thought of how I'd have to put it all back—ammonia, mop, bucket. Then it would start all over—paws, running shoes. I'd about talked myself out of washing the floor when the phone rang. It was my brother. "I want half," he said.

"Things get lost in the mail," I replied.

"Then send them UPS."

I told him about a UPS plane that had crashed outside of Tulsa, Oklahoma. He hung up.

Not long after, I received a letter from a lawyer directing me to send half our mother's ashes to Barnet. Or else.

"Or else, what?" I asked Hugh. "Will they throw me in jail, if I don't comply? I am not going to pack up half of Francine Bernstein's remains and send them to Barnet."

Shall I divide our mother with a measuring cup, the same cup I use to measure sugar and flour? I'd never be able to make another cake without thinking of her reduced to ashes. As it is, I think of her whenever I bake, though she comes to me full-blown. Alive. Recently, though, I made her chocolate cake, the one from the recipe on the Hershey's cocoa box and I knew she was dead. I didn't know it while I was making the cake, but after I tasted it, I told Hugh, "My mother is dead." It didn't taste like the cake she made for all our birthdays. Then I remembered the time mother said to Chubby Levine, "I thought you were making *my* sponge cake?" And Chubby said, "This *is* your sponge cake." Mother thought that was pretty funny, but I thought it was like asking a woman who isn't pregnant when her baby is due.

When our mother got sick, Barnet took control of her finances. When she was in the hospital, he wrote himself a big fat check and flew to Acapulco with his newest girlfriend. Then he bought a Cadillac SUV.

I told Hugh I believe in karma. "Look at Bernie Madoff." Then I rattled off the names of all the other connivers who ended up behind bars. Jeffrey Skilling. Michael Milken. Martha Stewart. That suave Indian who ran a hedge fund. The list gives me hope.

People do split ashes. My neighbor Caroline scattered half her mother under a rose bush, and now brilliant pink blooms are growing over the fence into my yard. She scattered the other half along the trail where she and her mother enjoyed walking. But I can't imagine my mother as compost and the only walks we ever took were up and down the aisles at Costco.

My friend Marsha's family scattered their mother all around the farm. They sprinkled some of her under the clothesline and recalled all the clothes she'd ever hung. They tossed a bit of her near the backyard swing and remembered the way she was always calling, "Watch out! You'll get kicked in the head!" They scattered her under the peace sign their father had painted on the side of the barn. There was even enough left for a grave. After the minister spoke, they each tossed some of their mother into it. Then they played a recording of her favorite Glenn Miller song, *Moonlight Serenade*, while sprinkling some of her favorite food on top of the ashes. Popcorn. Junior Mints. Potato chips.

I told Hugh, "Some families have all the fun."

*

In the beginning, he brought me cups of tea. He made pots of soup, rubbed my neck. Then he stopped. "There's grief," he said. "And then there's something else. I don't know what it is, but it isn't grief."

He said he'd never known me to be so unhappy. He even said it to Caroline, while she bent over her vegetable garden and attacked the weeds with a kitchen fork. He was standing over her, rubbing her dog's neck. I observed them from the back porch, where I'd gone searching for a book. I heard voices, so I went to the screen and there they were. I couldn't hear what they were saying because of a lawnmower off in the distance. Then the mower stopped and I heard Hugh say, "Vera is not happy."

His mother (*my* mother-in-law) is still alive. Ninety-three years old and mows her own lawn. The other day she spent four hours planting tulip bulbs. "What do *you* know of grief?" I asked him. "You've never lost anybody." Horrified, I clapped a hand to my mouth.

Hugh gave me a book: *The Grieving Process*, by Dr. H. M. Featherstone. According to Dr. Featherstone, I will react to my mother's death in stages. When I pass through the final stage, I will be ready, Dr. Featherstone assures me, "To jump back into the stream of life."

My grief, if that's what it is, doesn't comply with Dr. Featherstone's scheme. It comes in waves. It's messy. Unpredictable. Disorderly. I can be driving and suddenly it feels as if someone has dumped four sacks of potatoes in my lap. Once, while stopped at a traffic light, I realized there was no one to tell me to put on some lipstick. No one to say, *Do yourself a favor. Get rid of that old coat.* When the light changed, I couldn't move my foot from the brake to the gas pedal. Cars honked. Drivers yelled. I sat there and cried. Another time, I was on a garden tour when a woman said, "Smell this rose!" I thought she'd said, "Wake up and smell the roses," but then I saw her pointing to a trellis laden with blooms. I pressed my nose to a blossom and breathed in my Nonna's basement, which had reeked faintly of mildew and gas. Sometimes, I can be enjoying a meal and suddenly the food tastes as if I'm sucking on nickels.

The other day, I was out walking and the sight of some late-blooming phlox triggered a sense of despair so strong that I felt my knees buckle. It took all my will to keep moving. I couldn't recall any association with phlox. My mother hadn't gardened. Like me, she set a few pots of geraniums on the front stoop every spring. Yet something about the fading phlox behind a white picket fence made me weak in the knees. Or perhaps it was the weathered green and white striped cushions on wicker chairs arranged haphazardly on the front porch. The place looked like a home. Not the home I grew up in, but a home nevertheless. I wanted to go home. Only I couldn't.

When I tried describing the porch, the cushions, the phlox, Hugh said, "Home is where the heart is, Vera." I'd expected him to say, "You can't go home again." Either way, I was sorry I'd brought it up.

Is there really such a thing as too much grief, which is what Hugh is suggesting? Perhaps there's a grief gene, expressed in some kink on the strand of DNA that determines all ones other traits. My particulars include: washed out blonde hair; green eyes; short, stubby fingers; broad forehead; a slight bump at the bridge of my nose. No one has ever called me pretty. Interesting. Yes. Also lurking on that double helix that determined I would look interesting, not pretty, may be an over-expressed gene for grief.

My Nonna would have passed it on. Nonna grieved out loud. We'd be sitting around the dinner table—me, my mother, father, two brothers, Nonna—talking about the Cubs, or the stock market, or the tree that fell on the neighbor's car during last night's storm. Everyone would be talking at once. Then Nonna, who'd been quietly minding her own business, would lament, "Oy, Lou. Why did you die?" Just as suddenly, she'd sit back in her chair and fold her hands in her lap, like a cuckoo bird that retreats into its clock after heralding the hour. Before long, we stopped paying attention to Nonna's eruptions. Now, if Nonna were alive, I would say, *Tell me about your grief and I'll tell you about mine.* Back then, though, we kept on talking about falling trees, the tanking stock market. Someone always predicted that next year would be the year the Cubs would pull it off.

*

I was spritzing my wrists with perfume at the fragrance bar in Macy's when I heard someone say, "I have become the kind of woman who wears Enna Jetticks."

Crazy, but I thought it was my mother. It's easy to imagine her worrying that she'd become such a woman. She worried about everything. And she was always worrying out loud.

"In my next life," she'd say, as if she were a member of some esoteric Hindu sect, not a reformed Jew who attended synagogue once a year on the High Holy days. "In my next life, I'll be carefree. Lighthearted. I won't give a damn about anything, Vera. Just you wait and see." So it wasn't such a

154

leap to imagine my mother worrying out loud that she'd returned as the kind of woman who wore Enna Jetticks. Old lady shoes, she called them.

Not that the voice I heard was anything like my mother's, which was high-pitched and slightly nasal. The voice that carried down the length of the perfume bar was in a lower register. Finishing school came to mind. Summers in Nantucket. Locked jaw. What would such a woman know of Enna Jetticks? For that matter, what does anyone know of shoes that today might only be found on eBay?

The woman at the perfume bar who was not my mother had on strappy sandals with high heels and tiny gold buckles that fastened at the ankle. They were fire engine red.

Enna Jetticks were almost always black, though occasionally blue or beige. Most had laces and a modest, firm, broad heel. My first grade teacher wore black Enna Jetticks in winter, beige in autumn and spring. My father's secretary, Bunny Kohlberg, always wore Enna Jetticks, though you'd expect a woman named Bunny would wear a more playful shoe, a strappy red sandal, perhaps. Nobody in my family wore them. My aunts on my father's side—the Gabors, my mother called them—never left the house in anything but high heels. Every night, before bed, they moaned about their bunions and hammertoes while soaking their feet in tubs of hot water and Epsom salts. The women on my mother's side wore Capezios or Weejun loafers with knee socks, unless they were off to a wedding or bar mitzvah or a night on the town.

My eye traveled up from the red strappy sandals and followed the curve of the woman's calf to the point where her leg disappeared beneath a gay cotton skirt with a pattern of blowzy pink peonies. "A nice leg," I thought. My mother was always quick to remark on the shape of a leg. "She's a pretty woman," she'd say. "But get a load of those piano legs. Poor thing." Sometimes, out of the blue, she'd say, "You're lucky, kiddo. You've got nice legs. That's nothing to sneeze at." Later, I would study my legs in the bathroom mirror, trying to figure out what was nice about them. Or I'd try to figure out, for example, how the legs of a woman who'd sat across from me on the bus, had anything to do with the legs on my Aunt Vivian's Bechstein?

I spent much of my childhood trying to decipher my mother's remarks. "It was like learning to speak a foreign language," I told Hugh, early in our relationship, when I told him everything.

Turning my attention back to the fragrances in front of me, I spotted my mother's perfume. I dabbed some on my wrist to get a whiff of her heady, floral scent. After she died, I went through her closet, heaped her clothes on the floor and rolled around in them, hoping to soak up her essence. Later, I packed her clothes off to a women's shelter, but I kept her perfume. It's on my dresser, flanked by all the other bottles—Queen among the pawns. I never use it. Sometimes, though, I uncork the glass stopper and expect my mother to pop out of the bottle. Crazy. I know. Crazier still is that the perfume feels more real to me than her ashes, which are still on the living room mantle. How did Hugh put it? *Languishing.*

I set down the perfume and glanced again at the woman in the red shoes. She appeared to be in her mid-forties, like me. Her hair, a striking white blonde, was cropped short, showing off, to great effect, silver earrings the size of bangle bracelets. Other than a splash of color on her lips, she wore no makeup. She was pretty.

My mother was a bolder kind of pretty, like the peonies on the woman's skirt. Her hair was black. She wore it long, even at an age when most women lopped theirs off, as if they were entering a convent, not middle age. During the day, she controlled her hair with a plastic headband or a silver barrette, but at night she set it loose, like an animal that had been caged for too long. She smudged kohl around her eyes. And she always wore red lipstick, even when she cleaned the house. She played her beauty to the hilt, though she rued her legs, which were covered in a tangle of varicose veins. "Them's the breaks, kiddo," she'd say, as she held out a leg, studying it from this angle and that, while seated on the edge of the bed to put on her nylons.

The woman who was not wearing Enna Jetticks had smooth legs, though my mother would have found some flaw. If I were to say, "She has nice legs. Don't you think?" my mother would purse her lips and give me the stink eye. "Have I taught you nothing?" she'd say. "Look how bowed they are. Wait till she walks. You'll see. Rickets. They were probably too poor for milk when she was growing up. Her father drank the milk money." If I were to say, "How do you know all that?" she'd smile a crooked smile. "How do I know anything? Let's just say, 'I know.'" My mother was a firm believer in her own infallibility.

My cousin Simca called her a witch. "A good witch," she'd say. "Not the kind that eats children who get lost in the woods. Your mother knows things that other people don't know."

"She's just smart," I'd say, and Simca would shake her head and give me a baleful look. "You don't understand. Your mother knows things that nobody can possibly know. Not from books. Not from anything."

"You mean she has ESP?"

Simca sighed. "Oh, Vera, forget I said anything."

If my mother was so smart, why didn't she tell me what to do with her ashes? I read that Peggy Guggenheim gave instructions that she was to be buried with her Lhasa apsos in the garden of her palazzo on the Grand Canal. My mother, of course, hated dogs. "Why would anyone have an animal in the house?" she'd say. Still.

I considered asking the woman what she would do. But she and her red sandals had taken off. Vanished. Poof. Just like my mother. One day she was sitting up in bed telling me to get a mirror and her lipstick because the rabbi was on his way; next day she was gone. Later, when I told Hugh, "She could have given me some warning," he said, "She was very ill, Vera. How much warning did you need?"

Dr. Marx was no help. "Everyone's different," he'd said. "But Francine is remarkably resilient." Then he shrugged, held his hands out in an empty gesture, and said, "Your guess is as good as mine, Vera." While I appreciate a doctor who willingly acknowledges his own limitations, I felt troubled when Dr. Marx turned my mother's prognosis into a guessing game, one that I, an out-of-work teacher of English as a second language, might play as well as a medical specialist. *Guess how many jellybeans are in the jar! Guess what's behind Door Number Two! Guess when your mother will die!*

I glanced down the counter again, but the woman was still not there. I didn't need her advice. I've had enough of that. Simca suggested scattering my mother at Père Lachaise. "Near Jim Morrison's grave," she said. Simca dropped a lot of acid in college and followed The Doors everywhere. As far as I can tell, she's never regained her equilibrium. Even before that, my mother would say, "Vivian must have dropped Simca on her head when she was a baby."

Friends have suggested scattering my mother from a mountaintop. My Aunt Vivian told me about a charter boat that takes groups out to sea. When it drops anchor everyone tosses their loved ones' ashes overboard. It sounded like those Korean weddings where a thousand couples get married en masse. I told Vivian, "That's creepy." She agreed and confessed that her friend got into a fight with a man on the boat because he wore shorts and flip flops, and left his shirttails hanging out. "Your mother would have turned over in her grave at the sight of him," Vivian said. "That's the problem, Aunt Vivi. Mother isn't in a grave. Remem-

159

ber?" Then I reminded her that my parents had fought the day they were scheduled to buy their burial plots.

My mother's version of the story started with my father peering over the morning newspaper and saying, "Today's the day, Francine." When she said, "The day for what?" he reminded her they had an appointment to check out the plots. That's when she announced her plans for cremation. She reminded him that their tour guide, on the cruise they'd taken for their fortieth anniversary, had informed them that every plot on the Venetian burial island of San Michele had been spoken for years ago. New arrivals are dug up after ten years and moved to a common burial site farther out in the lagoon. "Venice!" Father exploded. "Are you cuckoo? This is Chicago. We have an option on two plots at Waldheim. Nobody is going to dig us up. Ever. Now go get ready, or we'll be late." Later, my mother confided, "Your father shouldn't have used the word 'ever.' I was already thinking of which handbag to use on our little outing. But the thought of spending eternity with him." She paused. "I can't explain it, but something came over me."

*

Now my mother is on the mantle wedged between a ceramic candleholder from Oaxaca and a wooden doll from an Indian tribe whose identity I no longer recall. The mantle is full of stuff I've carted home in suitcases. A crystal vase from the duty free shop in Dublin. A water jug from a potter at a street fair in Santa Fe. It's all there, in what Hugh calls, "Vera's pantheon of *tchotchkes*." I can pass by six times a day and never see any of it, not even my mother, whose remains are stored in a pretty tin box. Hugh is right. My mother is languishing.

The other day I came upon her while tearing the house apart in search of a cookbook, which I'd mislaid on the mantle. "Hey, Francine!" I said, pretending it really was my mother languishing in the tin box. But my mother was tall and full-figured. She had a presence. People looked up when she entered a room. The last time I saw her, she was sitting up in a hospital bed, telling me to get her lipstick. "Hurry," she said. "The rabbi will be here any minute." I held the mirror for her and when she was done coloring her lips, she said, "Now plump up my pillows, and find a way to dim the light. Nobody looks good in fluorescent."

When the rabbi arrived, I kissed her cheek and said I'd see her in the morning. Now she's in a tin box. "That's pretty weird," I told Hugh. "One minute, she's putting on lipstick for the rabbi, the next she's being vaporized in a sixteen hundred degree furnace, and then pulverized in a high-speed blender. And I'm supposed to believe that whatever is in this tin is my mother? For all I know, it might contain somebody else's ashes. Such things happen, you know."

I still haven't opened the tin. One afternoon, about two weeks after it arrived, I carried it into the living room, sat on the sofa, and poured myself a glass of wine. With each sip I promised myself that before the next sip, I would lift the lid. But I couldn't stop thinking of Pandora.

*

And then I thought of Lillian and the afternoon I ran into her, on my way back from the *mercado*. This was years ago. Her eyes were red from crying; her cheeks were streaked with blue mascara. Even her hair, which ordinarily covered her head like a protective shell, a blonde, lacquered carapace, had collapsed. "Bobbie died," she said.

Bobbie was a yappy white terrier who had gone everywhere with Lillian. She kept him tethered to a baby blue, leather lead, though sometimes, like a French woman, she tucked him into her handbag. Lillian was from Teaneck, New Jersey.

I hugged Lillian and offered to escort her back to her place, which was also mine. We were both renting rooms for the winter from the Aguados—Rafael and Lolita—who owned a rambling home on a dusty road in San Miguel. Their place was about a fifteen-minute walk from the Plaza Civica and even farther from the bougainvillea-covered tourist posadas that looked like money. Lillian refused my offer. "I took a valium," she said.

Lillian was not the kind of woman who evoked pity. Once, I'd stopped her in the Aguados' courtyard to ask directions to a *panaderia* she'd been raving about. She started to explain, then stopped, looked at me, as if for the first time, and said, "If you ever expect to find a husband, you'd better do something with your hair." Still, that afternoon, as she blew her nose into a shredded tissue, I felt sorry for her. I felt even sorrier for Bobbie, though I hadn't liked him. He was an exotic breed, with white extravagant fur that frizzed around him like cotton candy. He yipped and cried on the rare occasions when Lillian left him alone. In the mornings, he chased after Lourdes, the young girl who cleaned our rooms, nipping at her ankles.

After Lillian and I parted, I slipped into a small church and lit a candle for Bobbie. As I watched the flame flicker then bloom, I repented for ever having called Bobbie the Devil Dog, if only under my breath. I also prayed that I would not be punished for impersonating a woman of faith, a woman of a *different* faith, one who had no business standing before a shrine to Santa Rita lighting a candle for a dead dog. Then, audaciously, I crossed myself, following the example of the woman who had preceded me at the altar.

A few days later, I watched through my window as Lillian tended the flowers outside her room, which like mine, faced the courtyard. I was waiting to catch her do something. But what? Sob and fling herself in despair onto the ground? Kiss Bobbie's baby blue leash? Fill his water bowl, which she kept outside her door? Instead, she did ordinary things like press a finger into the flowerpots to test for moisture. She deadheaded some marigolds and moved a potted begonia out of the sun. Then she looked around, as if she sensed someone was watching her. Foolishly, I ducked behind the curtain, but she saw me and waved, motioning for me to come out and join her.

When I asked how she was doing, she ignored me and continued watering a Bird of Paradise. I was beginning to think that I'd only imagined she'd beckoned me, when she set down the watering can and said, "Come inside and see Bobbie."

Lillian had a deluxe room. Unlike mine, hers had a kitchen and a capacious living room. "He's over there," she said, pointing to the mantle above the adobe fireplace. The mantle was lined with blue and white ceramic mugs and plates, the kind you can pick up in the *mercado* for a song. I scanned the mantle not knowing what to say. I thought that Lillian had gone off the rails. Then, just as I was about to pretend that I saw her poor mutt lurking amid the crockery, she plucked a shiny object from the mantle. It looked like a tennis ball can that had been sprayed with silver paint. "He's in here," she said. "Bobbie's in here." She held the can close to her cheek and kissed it. "Such a little dog," she said. "And so many ashes. How can that be?"

When I asked what she planned to do with his ashes, she backed away from me, hugged the can to her breast, gave me a fierce look and said, "How did you get in here?"

I don't know what became of Lillian and Bobbie. Perhaps he's still on the mantle. More likely, Lillian took him home to New Jersey. By now, Lillian may be on a mantle somewhere. That all happened so long ago, before I met Hugh and settled down. It happened, as my mother would say, *long before moveable type.*

*

"A tour bus driver stopped me and asked, 'Are you from here?'" Hugh pauses and looks around the table, gauging his audience. I've heard this story. He told it at dinner the night he returned from his meeting.

He's embellishing now. Or else I've forgotten this particular detail—that the driver had an English accent. Perhaps I spaced out when he told it the first time. Lately, he's been accusing me of that. Spacing out. More likely, I received the abridged version, the energy-saving iteration of a story that, either way, isn't worth stopping a dinner party in its tracks to tell. Before Hugh grabbed the spotlight, the guests, eight in all, were talking in little groups. The room buzzed with their chatter, reminding me of my neighbor Caroline's bees. Then Hugh cleared his throat and launched into his story—the unabridged version. When it had been just the two of us, he must have done some mental calculation, the kind he does for a living, and decided there was no need to squander his energy on me. Now he's the SUV he rails against, the energy hog releasing too many hydrocarbons into the air. He repeats the bus driver's question, this time with an English accent. Then he says, "We were in *New* England, for God's sake." He's shaking his head in faux bemusement, signaling that laughter would be appropriate since after all, he had not been in *England*. He'd been to a meeting of other carbon offset calculators. They hold their gatherings in expensive, inaccessible venues. This one was on an island. "We were in *New* England," he repeats, with another shake of his head.

Colin, the lawyer for Hugh's non-profit, is sneaking a look at his watch, and Susannah, the group's web guru, just telegraphed a desperate look to her husband across the table. Hugh, undeterred, is barreling ahead. "I told the driver that I was just visiting. Nevertheless, he said, 'Do you happen to know if John Belushi is buried at the cemetery down the road?'"

The British accent is getting on my nerves. After the guests are gone, I'll say something. *You sounded like Sasha Baron Cohen impersonating a Russian oligarch.* Hugh will groan. *I was that bad?* I'll nod and he'll laugh and I'll laugh, and then we'll finish our nightcaps and toddle off to bed. No. I won't say anything. Not tonight.

He's still holding forth. "Of course, I said that I didn't know where Belushi is buried. But then, get a load of this, the driver said, 'Oh. That's okay. I'll assume that he is.'"

An uncomfortable silence settles over the table. When Hugh told me the story, I said, "*Assume?* You don't think he actually drove by the cemetery and announced that John Belushi is buried there?"

Now the man seated to my right—I've forgotten his name—hits the rim of his plate with the base of his wine glass, which he has just drained for the third, or possibly the fourth, time. Meanwhile, Hugh's story hovers over the table like an auction item for which nobody has offered a starting bid. I must break the silence. I catch Hugh's gaze and say, "You don't think that he drove by the cemetery and announced that John Belushi is buried there?"

For my effort I receive a withering look, the look Hugh has sent at countless dinner parties, the one suggesting I might not want to pour another glass of wine. Only this look doesn't feel protective. He is reprimanding me for speaking out of turn, for rushing in before any of our guests—*his* co-workers, dullards every one—has had a chance to speak. Why do I feel as if I've helped myself to the hors d'oeuvres before all our guests have been served?

I return Hugh's look with a shrug, then continue. "It makes you wonder if you can trust anyone. Or any *thing*. I mean, here are all these people, paying good money for a tour, and their guide is making things up. Dare I say, *lying?*"

In the right setting, my remark might trigger a discussion of trust. Trust in government. Trust in your fellow man. *Or woman*, I might add, should the conversation take that turn. Who can you trust these days? *What* can you trust? Can you trust that your government isn't spying on you? Or that your pilot has landed the plane many times before, but not so many that he's too old to be flying? For that matter, can you trust that your husband hasn't fallen for your neighbor, the one who has become a beekeeper? There was something about the way he chatted with Caroline the other day, the way he stood there rubbing her dog's neck while she weeded her tomato plants with a kitchen fork.

But the conversation doesn't turn to trust. Instead, Colin asks Hugh, "Is he?"

"Is he what?" Hugh sounds peeved. It's the tone he reserves for me whenever I challenge him. Once, I suggested that buying carbon offsets is not unlike buying indulgences for absolution. "The rich can pollute, then buy a tree and feel absolved," I'd said. He didn't speak to me for days.

Colin is trying to clear up the confusion. "I mean, is John Belushi buried in that cemetery?"

When Hugh shrugs, the lawyer says, "Well, I suppose you didn't have time to go look for the grave."

It is a statement that can be read either way. Colin may be acknowledging that Hugh had more important things to do. Or perhaps he's suggesting that Hugh lacks curiosity. I'm putting my money on the latter.

I'd asked the same question, more or less. "Did you go to the cemetery?"

"Why would I do that?" he'd replied.

When I said, "Why do we do anything?" he accused me of being "too existential."

"But your little tale does raise the matter of existence," I'd said. "Didn't the bus driver say, '*Are you from here?*'"

If the assembled weren't such dullards, I'd try to revive the conversation along such lines. Instead, I hear myself saying, "My mother didn't want to be buried." Suddenly, I'm launching into the tale of how, on the day she and my father were scheduled to buy their burial plots, she announced her intention to be cremated. "If my mother were buried," I tell the assembled, "I could visit her grave. Lay flowers beside it. Set stones on her marker. Instead, she is languishing on the mantle. That's what Hugh says. 'Just leave your mother to languish on the mantle, Vera.' But really, if my mother is languishing, it's her own fault."

Nobody is checking a phone, consulting a watch. I have everybody's attention when I say, "Peggy Guggenheim specified that she was to be buried with her Lhasa apso's in the garden of her palazzo on the Grand Canal. I bet you didn't know that."

In one of my V-8 talks, the talks I imagine I'd had with my mother when she was alive, I tell her about Peggy Guggenheim and her dogs. Then I say, *And you? What are your wishes?* Of course, true to form, she replies, *I can't see why anyone would have an animal in the house. I certainly don't want to be buried with one. Honestly, Vera, you take the cake.* Then I explain that the Lhasa apso story was only an example. *It would just help,* I say, *if you could tell me what you want me to do. With you.*

But the matter of her ashes never came up. We talked about everything but dying, unless you count the time she said, *I suppose I had a good life.* Only in one of my V-8 talks did I think to say, *Tell me more.*

*

When Simca suggested Père Lachaise I said my mother never shared her enthusiasm for The Doors. Then the next day, while going through my mother's belongings, I found a satin handbag. Inside, in florid script, a small tag read, *Paris, France.* It felt like a sign.

The bag has a delicate golden chain to wrap around your wrist. A spray of flowers is stitched to one side. Why does the word posy come to mind? *Ring around the rosie. A pocketbook full of posies.* Or ashes. I've considered packing my mother in it. But it may be too small, even though my mother, who was forever dieting to lose the same twelve pounds, has been reduced to a mere four pounds of ash.

The satin bag has a small zippered compartment in which I discovered a tissue. My mother's lips are on it, blotted in red. Funny, but that lipstick stain feels more real to me than her vaporized, pulverized remains.

I even found a penny in the bag. *A penny for your thoughts.* I never said that to her. Not even when she was in the hospital and said, "I suppose I've had a good life." I remember there was resignation in her voice, as if she were telling the butcher, *I suppose that rump roast on the end will do.*

She'd been sitting up in bed reading the newspaper and I was sitting across from her knitting a scarf for Hugh. I remember dropping a stitch and saying, "Crap." Then I picked up the stitch and finished the row. I never picked up on my mother's remark.

If that had been me sizing up *my* life, Dr. Becker, the therapist Hugh found for me, would say, "*Suppose?* Aren't you sure that your life was good?" Then there'd be a long silence, during which time I would be wondering whether Dr. Becker counts the minutes waiting for me to speak. Or I would calculate the cost of saying nothing. Or I'd try to guess the cost of the shoes Dr. Becker tucks beneath the chair that she sits upon lotus style. Then she would say, "The hour is up, Vera. We'll take this up next time."

I thought there'd be a next time when I gave my mother a swift kiss on the cheek and said I'd return in the morning. When I asked if she wanted anything from the outside world, she said, "Paul Newman." We laughed. At least there was that. A last laugh.

But I never cut through to her when she had a voice. I never said, *Aren't you sure that your life was good?* Now I have conversations with her in my head. I call them my V-8 talks. Hugh thinks that sounds like a summit meeting of the Western Allies. "It's nothing like that," I told him. I asked if he remembered the commercial where a man drinks a sugary beverage, then slaps his forehead and says, "I could have had a V-8!" That's what I do. I slap my forehead and say, *I could have said this when she was alive. I could have said that.*

There were so many times when I could have said this or that, like that day in the hospital when she read the paper and I knitted. I remember at one point, she said, "Get a load of this." Then she tossed the paper aside. "Oh, never mind." She sighed and flopped back into the pillows. "The Republicans exhaust me. I won't miss them."

"Are you going somewhere?"

"Honestly, Vera. You take the cake."

"You said, 'I won't miss them,' implying…"

"Implying nothing. When those bums are voted out of office, I won't miss them. End of story."

Now, in my V8 talks, I say things like, *There's more to the story.* Sometimes I ask if she's afraid. Predictably, she says, *Afraid of what?* To which I reply, *You know. Dying.* And then she says, *Who said anything about death?*

That's how it would have gone, even if I *had* talked to her when she had a mouth.

Now I imagine her walking into the store where she bought the satin handbag, selecting it from among all the others, one prettier than the next. What was she wearing that day? What day? What was I doing when she walked into that shop? And where is it? So many questions. Why didn't I ask them when I could?

When I told Hugh I was going to Paris, I didn't tell him that I plan to find the shop, though by now it's probably a Benetton or a Gap. But if it's still there, I intend to find it. Then I'll stroll in with my mother dangling from my wrist by a golden chain and I'll say, "I bet you didn't expect to see this place again, Francine. Did you?"

"Pocket Full of Posies" originally appeared in *Passages North.*

Black Velvet Band

by Karen McIntyre

For years after, when he told this story, Jimmy would say he knew the day was fucked when he saw the old man waiting outside the bar. Eight-thirty in the morning, he'd say, and there was old Mr. Edwards shaking in his tan raincoat, no match for the March wind trying to blow him into his grave. The neighborhood around Fitzy's was no treat on the brightest of mornings. Under that gray and hopeless sky, the little wooden houses with their sagging porches, one yard with a plastic Santa still waving from his sled— well, it was enough to make Jesus Himself reach for the Jameson's bottle.

Jimmy wasn't supposed to let anyone in before he set up his cash drawer, filled the ice bins, and all the other small, rattling tasks it took to get the bar on its feet for another long day. But Mr. Edwards was one of Fitzy's favorites. Everyone knew that. And so Jimmy picked up his pace, limping slightly, past the weedy lot to the corner where Fitzy's

Irish Pub squatted in its low brick building. There were shamrocks in the window for St. Patrick's Day, and a chalkboard sign chained by one leg where Fitzy, the owner, had written, "Irish Flu Shots, $3" in green chalk, just beginning to blur.

When the old man saw Jimmy, he raised his newspaper in salute, and Jimmy gave a tight, businesslike nod in return, as if they were colleagues passing in the corridor of a bank somewhere, and Jimmy took the ring of keys from his jacket and opened the heavy front door. Even in those days, Fitzy's was old school. Dim light and dark wood and that smell in the air. The ghost of ancient beer spills and cigarettes long exhaled.

Jimmy went behind the bar and found a fresh can of V-8. Eight vegetables? Jimmy hoped they were in there, for Mr. Edwards's sake. Vodka, vodka, vodka, a full three-second pour. Salt. Pepper. A squeeze of lime for the vitamin C. Skip the horseradish, the poor bastard's belly took enough of a beating. He watched Mr. Edwards pulled the pale red liquid through a straw into his scarecrow body, his hands pressed down firm on the bar but still shaking as if small animals were trapped under his palms trying to escape.

He'd forgotten to lock the door behind them. The man walked right in.

The man was heavy, but not yet fat, in a down vest zipped tight and belled out over the tight cinch of his belt. Small eyes were set deep in the pudge of his face, like two nails hammered in.

"Come back in an hour," Jimmy said. "We're not open yet."

The man just stood there with his feet planted far apart on the tiles. "You look open to me. Any coffee?"

Jimmy folded his arms over his chest.

"Nah, never mind, when in Rome, and all that," the man said. "I'll take a Miller draft."

Jimmy smiled as he pulled the Miller tap, knowing the hose ran down to the basement and into a keg of Kohler beer, the cheapest in the discount warehouse. He tipped the glass to get the head just right and held it up to admire the fizzing gold.

"A fine crackery finish with just a trace of paint thinner," he said, and rang up seven dollars for a five-dollar draft. Asshole surcharge. Fitzy would understand.

Erin, the day waitress, didn't like the looks of the man either. "Did you see him before, jotting notes in his wee notebook?"

"Looking at us like we're thieves," Jimmy said.

"Well you, anyway." She peered up at Jimmy. She was a young woman, almost pretty, dressed trim and tidy with her apron tied tight. A long brown braid down her back and startling light eyes with dark rings around the iris, like a husky. "Not to get your knickers in a twist. Just to be watchful and wary."

"I'm always wary," he said.

"Of course you are. Now mind that mess down there." She pointed at the clutter of glasses the night man had left at the end of the bar. Fitzy liked to run a tight ship, and Erin would be the first to tell.

Schiff and the guys from the highway crew clomped in, wearing bright orange vests over their heavy work clothes.

"Hi honey, I'm home," Schiff called out.

Jimmy was already working the tap. "I was getting worried," he said, "you might've actually finished that road by now."

Schiff took a long drink, the muscles of his throat working. He was a big man with cheeks boiled red from being out in the cold all night. He looked at the man sitting in the corner by himself.

"Who's the new boy?" he asked.

The man hopped off his stool and stuck out his hand.

"I'm Dan," he said.

"Dan the man!" Schiff shouted in his friendly way. He took another long pull on his beer. "Hey Jimmy. What happened to my Bruins last night?"

"I couldn't watch," Jimmy said. "What a gong show."

"That pussy Doughty went out for a muscle pull?" Schiff said. "In my day they played with broken bones."

Dan hovered at Schiff's elbow, looking from one face to another. "I never got into hockey," he said, like it was a virtue.

Ignore him, Jimmy wanted to say. Though when Schiff found a new audience there was no stopping him.

"Football. Baseball. Basketball." Schiff ticked them off on his thick fingers. "What do they all have in common?

They play on turf. Or a field. Or a nice wooden floor." In his Boston accent it came out *flah*.

"Hockey? Hockey! They're playing on a sheet of fucking *ice*!" He poked Dan in the chest. "You tell me what's hahdah!"

"Well the athleticism may be superior, I grant you that," Dan said. Jimmy wanted to punch him in the squinty eye. You want hockey? *There's hockey.*

"That you?" The man pointed with his chin at the framed black-and-white photo behind the bar. Jimmy didn't turn. He didn't let himself look at it more than once or twice a day. It was a good picture, the kind that jumped out at you from the sports section. He was skating just ahead of the pack, leaning forward with his stick outstretched, the puck and everything else still just ahead of him.

He started to mutter something to shut it down, to shut the asshole up, but Schiff was all over it, feeling the glow of his second beer, going on about how Jimmy was the *man*, a playmaker, the star on that miserable frat-boy college team, not like the pussies who were afraid to mix it up. Jimmy went down the bar, cleaning glasses, not wanting to hear it or explain what the doctor said, or whether he could *coach*, for Chrissake, like anyone would hire him.

By now, Billy the cop had come in, and a jostling rowdy group from the EJ factory, and they were thronged around the bar, the place filling up with bodies and the deep voices of men.

"Oh Billy," Mr. Edwards called down the bar. Jimmy came over and refilled his empty glass. He never corrected the old man, not since that first week after he moved out of his dorm room, his belongings stuffed into Hefty bags, and took the job at Fitzy's because it was offered him. Mr. Edwards came in every day wearing the same worn suit, but his watch showed the right time and his shirt was always clean. He spent his days gazing across the bar, his face alternately lighting and fading, drinking and drinking but never getting drunk, just sinking slowly through the day like a ship taking on water until he left finally at three or four in the afternoon with that slow, straight-backed walk, Jimmy's hand on his arm, out the heavy front door to the cab they would call for him.

Mr. Edwards fished in his wallet and pulled out a rumpled five. He dug his hands in his pockets and slapped a few coins on the bar.

"It's ok," Jimmy said.

"No, Billy, I've got it, son." Mr. Edwards pulled a white windowed envelope from his pocket and tried to extract the social security check from inside.

Jimmy took the envelope, smoothed it, and put it back in the old man's hand. "Put that away. You can run a tab."

"I can?"

"Yes."

"What did you say?"

He talked low into the old man's pink ear, which smelled faintly of corn chips. "A tab. TAB."

178

Mr. Edwards's blinked his watery blue eyes. Jimmy took the old man's glass and tapped the bar in front of him. "Another?"

"You're a kind man and a gentleman, Billy," Mr. Edwards said in that way you couldn't tell was sarcastic or sincere, or maybe confusing Jimmy with his grown son who didn't talk to him anymore. No matter, it was still a nice thing to say.

Down the bar, Dan pushed his own glass forward. "I'll take another. And you can run a tab for me, too."

"Sure, let's see your credit card."

"What? You didn't ask him for one."

"I know him," Jimmy said.

"You know me too. You know damn well who I am," the man said.

Schiff took a pile of folded bills from his Carhart overall. "Hey, let me get this round."

"No." Jimmy pushed Schiff's money back at him. "He can pay."

Dan stood up, struggling into his tight down vest. "You know, I try to be nice, and this is where it gets me. I can make your life a lot less pleasant, let me tell you."

"Now now," Schiff said.

"I'll be back," the man said. "And your boss will be hearing about it, too."

"My boss," Jimmy snorted.

"Yes sir, this will all be taken into account. I know when I'm being disrespected."

He stepped backward and knocked into Schiff, who tried to right him with a hand on his arm but he twisted away, lost his balance and grabbed the bar stool. It went over, CRACK! on the tile floor, and the men all stood watching, drinks half raised.

"I'm fine," Dan said. "What'd you put in my beer?"

"Uh … beer?" Jimmy said, and the men looked this way and that, trying not to laugh in this other man's face. He made it to the door and gave it a mighty shove that got him nowhere, because it needed a pull. Which, he reminded them, was against the fire codes, and they listened in silence until he finished his speech about how even a shithole should be a law-abiding shithole, and then he left.

Lunchtime. Someone had fed the jukebox and an Irishman was singing about a dark-eyed girl who'd led him away from home and into a lonely prison cell. Jimmy padded up and down the bar, pointing at empty glasses, and the man would either shake his head and hoist himself off the bar stool or nod and Jimmy would grab the bottle from the speed rack and move it up and down for a generous pour, then a fizz of soda from the gun to make it a cocktail instead of a vice, and the clatter and clink of cutlery and the kitchen door swinging open and shut and Eduardo, the busboy, going back and forth with an armful of dishes and his smooth, dark face with its faraway look, and Erin squeezing between the coats draped over the back of chairs and stepping nimbly over the backpacks and pocketbooks and briefcases people left on the floor to set the heavy white platters on the tables, laden with shepherd's pie and fish and chips and hamburgers with thick golden fries. All the while, the Irish Rovers singing *I thought she was queen o' the land, her hair hung over her shoulders, tied up with a black velvet band.* The pouncing, lilting rhyme insisting its way into every ear, so all up and down the bar, fingers tapped and below it, on the brass rail, feet moved up and down, in mud-caked work boots or sneakers or shoes, all keeping time to the beat.

Courtney came in after the rush, shaking her bright blond hair.

"Well, Daddy wants to know, should he talk to his friend?" she asked.

"I don't want him to go to trouble," Jimmy said.

"It won't be trouble. Unless you fuck up," Courtney said. Erin walked past, eyes down on the plate in her hand.

"Do we have to talk about this now?" he asked. "Here?"

She flipped her hair and smoothed it back down so the blunt shining ends lined up against her sweater. "So when *is* a good time, that's my question."

And then it started, Courtney going on about how her poor dad saw Jimmy as almost a kind of son, almost, and the thought of it began to squeeze at him, picturing Mr. Williams at the barbecue grill poking the meat with his gut sticking out and that look on his face. There was a bottle cap caught in the treads of the black bar mat under Jimmy's feet and it became a game, to see if he could kick it out with just the toe of his sneaker, and he realized too late she had gone quiet, in fact the whole bar had gone quiet, and he picked his head up to see her flushed face and the tears welling up over her eyeliner.

"Court," he said. "Court, please." He handed her a square white bar napkin.

She dabbed at the wing of her liner.

"I appreciate everything," he said. "I just don't want you to ask your dad before—before I know what I want to do."

"Fine," she said. "I won't help."

"Good," he said. "That's a good plan."

In the quiet part of the afternoon Jimmy spread the *Sun Herald* out on the bar and smoothed it open to the classified section. He touched the point of his pen down the row to the ad that said "Route Sales" and filled in the R and the o and the top of the small e, trying to think what it would feel like to want to drive a truck with "Martin's Potato Rolls" blaring from the side, that even in this crap town, some kid would tag with graffiti. Put on a uniform that said, this is it, this is my life, and jockey a hand truck loaded with hamburger buns through a jingling front door, then kneel in an aisle putting them away while people moved around you, shopping, looking down at your bent back.

He looked up to see Erin watching. She had one half-empty ketchup bottle stacked on top of another, the glass openings touching while ketchup glopped slowly down from one bottle to the other. He made as if to knock them with his hand but she grabbed his wrist, strong and quick.

"You'd have made a hell of a goalie," he said.

She nodded at the paper. "I thought Courtney's dad was going to hook you up with a guy."

He flapped the paper shut. "I'm not driving a bread truck." Quick he snatched the ketchup bottle from her hand and lobbed it into the recycle bin. It clanked hard against the beer bottles but did not break.

"You're a bit of an asshole," Erin said.

"You started it."

He watched her roll a fork and a knife into a paper napkin and drop it into the gray plastic tray with the others awaiting the dinner service. "Me, I'm going to BCC. They have a two-year program to be an X-ray tech. Why are you laughing at me?"

He made himself stop. "No, I think it's cute."

"The hospital is always hiring, I'm practically guaranteed a job when I get out."

"That's what you want?" he asked. "People's bones."

"When you—" she pointed at his ankle—"had your situation there, do you remember your x-ray tech?"

"I remember nothing." It was almost true. Lights smeared through a rainy windshield and the shattering of glass, his leg, everything.

"They're almost always nice people. And you know, the guidance counselor lady told me, lots of athletes study physical therapy. You could be helping people. Use your strength, help them walk again."

"I do that now," he said. "You just described my job to me."

She rolled the last knife and fork, dashed it into the plastic tray and turned away, braid swinging.

"Hold on." He grabbed her arm. "I'm happy for you. Let's have a drink, you and I. Celebrate."

"Oh," she said. "It's not going to be that kind of day."

"You're no fun," he said.

She looked at him a long moment. "Think you have enough fun in your life, wouldn't you say?"

God only doled out one first sip a day, and so Jimmy closed his eyes to the yeasty brightness fizzing over his tongue and opening out inside him, promising an ease and carefree it never quite delivered but still, it never hurt to try. He set the empty glass on the bar, meeting Erin's eyes for just the moment it took for her to sigh and turn her face away.

He poured an inch of Jameson's. Just an inch. Took a sip and looked into the glass. Put it down. Picked it up and drank it off to feel the warmth sluice down and spread through him, the pain in his leg receding and what was so wrong with that? The Irishman was singing about the girl again. That kind of day.

"All right, keep an eye, okay?" he asked Erin. The bar was almost empty. Just Mr. Edwards and a few guys from the law firm on State Street. He took his pack of Marlboros from behind the bar.

The day came at him in a rush of sun and cold, bringing water to his eyes. Broken glass glittered from the empty lot across the street. A pickup truck rattled past. He stood inhaling the smoke and freezing air deep into his lungs, his bad leg propped up on the building behind him.

Bartending wasn't a bad job. It was dead end, sure, but in a way that said, there are places I'd rather be, I'm just not ready to go there yet. He had that idea for a movie about a guy who won a scholarship and was on his way to the majors, then broke his ankle and lost it all—it made him cry when he'd told Fitzy, and Fitzy had thumped him hard on the chest, so hard he'd backed up a step and bumped into the edge of the bar. *Heart of a lion*, Fitzy had roared, *that's what you call it!* It was a good story, everyone said. It only needed to be written, and how hard could that be? Plus, when you were a bartender, you controlled the alcohol, so even though you were waiting on people, they respected you. The lawyers in suits. The businesswomen who came in for a glass of wine and stayed through dinner, picking at French fries. *It was supposed to be* my *weekend with the kids*, they'd say. Or, *I guess I'm the only one in the office who can refill the damn paper tray.* And he'd take their glass and dash the dregs in the sink and give them a fresh one filled to the brim, on the house, and they'd lift their cup of kindness with a look that was surely real happiness, what else could you call it? Fitzy always said, it was a sacred public service they performed, saving their people from drinking alone.

A blue Oldsmobile pulled up across the street and a man got out. Jimmy knew him, just from the plant of his feet and the bulk of his vest. Another man got out on the passenger side and stood looking at him over the hood of the car. He was a big man wearing a leather jacket and a

185

blank, hard look. Jimmy stubbed his cigarette against the brick of the building and carried it inside to throw away.

Mr. Edwards was still sitting quietly at the bar and Jimmy put a hand on his thin shoulder as he passed, and Mr. Edwards raised his own gnarled hand and gave him a pat, and Jimmy went behind the bar, took the bills from the tip cup, and tapped them straight against the bar. In an hour, the light outside would fade and Sal, the night man, would take over, making his way down the bar, *hey chief, hey boss, how's it going, what'll it be?* And it did seem like any other Tuesday, as if Fitzy would walk through the door any minute now, in his old corduroy jacket with the pockets stuffed full of bills and receipts, and head back behind the bar to slap the register open and poke at the cash drawer with a grunt and a nod. But Fitzy would not be coming through that door anymore. He was gone, dead and in the ground at Gate of Heaven cemetery out on Route 12, past where the General Electric plant used to be. And though the corporation that had bought the bar from his widow would keep his name above the door, for all the dark wood and music it was a place without a soul and everyone could feel it.

Dan had come in with the hard-faced man. They stood at the end of the bar watching Jimmy. "When you get a chance," Dan said. "We'd like some service down here."

Jimmy picked up a glass. Swished it in the rinse water and stacked it on the rack.

"See?" the man said to his friend. "That attitude. Well guess what, there'll be some changes here. No more so-called tabs for these so-called customers you know damn well will never be able to pay. And no more of how you do your so-called 'restocking,' I've seen the funnels and the jugs of warehouse gin, you think I was born yesterday?"

"Let's not get into how you were born," Jimmy said.

The men standing around them didn't move. Still, there was that sense of them drawing together, watching.

"I've had just about enough of your attitude," Dan said.

Jimmy felt it then. The *whoosh* of rightness he used to feel on the ice when he knew without thinking how the action would turn, skating fast and free into the clack of the puck against his stick, the crowd shouting around him. He took the keys from his jacket and dropped them on the bar.

Later, he'd tell the story from behind the bar at O'Malley's, then at Sullivan's, and finally at his own place down on Water Street, a snug little tavern with dark wood and cozy lamps, like a rich man's library, he liked to think, the kind of place you could sit for hours and ride out a wintry day. And later he would say, putting on Fitzy's brogue, *'twas the only sound in the place, it was. Not a cough, not a foot shuffle or the sound of the Gent's room flushing, just the sweet jingle of those keys hitting the good old wood of the bar,* and the men gathered around would nod, seeing it too, the sound of his voice like music.

A Mouth is a House for Teeth

by Michelle Ross

The mother is never to answer the door. If there's a knock, she is to hide. She is to hide herself and the girl, make it appear that no one is home. Unless the knock is the husband's secret knock that only the two of them know. Then she is to open the door. There's a keyhole, of course, but the husband doesn't take the key with him when he's away. For starters, carrying a key is a nuisance. Second, why does he need to carry a key if she is always home? Third, and most important, what if someone who wishes to hurt the girl and the mother steals the key from the husband and lets himself into the house?

The outside is dangerous to the girl, and by proxy, dangerous to the mother. In truth, the outside would be dangerous to the mother even if she were not a mother, but because there is the child, the mother is particularly vulnerable.

The only time she should ever open the door other than when she hears the secret knock that only she and the husband know is when there is a supply drop. She knows supplies have arrived because she hears the supply box thunk the concrete. She knows the thunk is the supply box because she schedules the delivery of the supply boxes, and always the boxes show up at the exact second they are scheduled.

Now, for instance. She hears the scheduled thunk. She looks through the peephole and sees the box, its dimensions distorted by the peephole's fisheye lens. She opens the door. There before her is the box.

There before her is also a decapitated head of a rabbit, a few inches from the box. It's shriveled, old. Through the peephole, she assumed it was a rock that had gotten kicked up by wind, whether natural or drone-created. Actually, perhaps the truth is she didn't think anything of it at all.

Now, the dead rabbit's dull black eyes seem to stare at her feet. She looks around, but she sees no one, not even the drone that delivered the box, not even her closest neighbor, who is not a mother of a young child, and who, therefore, is free to go outside as she pleases. What the mother does see is the street, the street that goes for miles and miles and that connects to other streets that go for miles and miles. Like a capillary in a network of blood vessels that circuit the continent. Follow it, and you can go anywhere. She feels the pull of the street. Or maybe this pull is just hormones. She knows better than to trust hormones. Hormones are how she got here in the first place.

She drags the supply box into the house and quickly closes and locks the door. She looks through the peephole at the rabbit head that looks like a stone. The mother doesn't hear the girl approach. The girl says, "Daddy home?" and the mother screams.

When the girl cries, the mother hugs her. "Sorry, I didn't know you were there. It's just the supply box. See?"

"When is Daddy coming home?" the girl asks.

"Like I've told you, Baby. I don't know."

"When's he going to call?"

"I don't know. Let's see about breakfast, OK?"

The girl returns to her bedroom, shuts the door.

The mother looks out the peephole again. The rabbit head is gone.

She puts her hand on the knob, thinks of opening the door to be sure the rabbit head wasn't just blown closer to the door where the fisheye can't reach. But to open the door again, when she has already dragged in the supply box, would be breaking protocol.

As long as they follow protocol, they are safe. The girl is safe. The mother is safe. The husband has told her this hundreds of times.

She takes her hand off the door.

*

When the husband is away, there is no certainty of when he will return. There is no certainty he will return at all. This is basic common sense and would be so even if the husband's work wasn't dangerous, which it is. It would be common sense even if he could talk openly to the mother and the girl about his work, which he cannot. Sometimes when the husband has had a drink and is feeling good, he might say, like they do in the movies, "I'd tell you, but then I'd have to kill you." Then he laughs. Or he doesn't.

It's been five days now since the husband last called. This is not unusual. When he doesn't call for several days, sometimes the mother imagines the husband is dead. She wonders how much time will pass before someone informs her.

Sometimes when he does call, like he does today when she and the girl are eating blueberry pancakes, and says, "It's been a really tough week" and "Man, am I exhausted," and doesn't ask how she's doing, she wishes he were dead.

When the girl was born, the husband was always finding excuses to leave the house. They needed more diapers. They needed more crackers. The car needed a full detail and wax.

She says, "Before you go, I need to tell you something. There was a rabbit head next to the supply box this morning."

"A what?"

"A decapitated rabbit head," she says.

The girl pays close attention.

The mother continues. "And then, barely a minute later, when I looked out the peephole, the rabbit head was gone."

"Probably a hawk or a cat," the husband says.

"That decapitated it or that hauled it away as soon as I dragged in the supply box?"

"Both?" he says. "I'm sure it's nothing to worry about. You're following protocol?"

She says, "Of course."

"Then you have nothing to worry about," he says.

"The head was shriveled, old," she says.

"Probably the wind lifts it as easily as a pebble." The husband asks the girl how she's doing.

The girl says, "I had to get an antibiotic. I had an infection in my leg."

The husband, who seconds earlier seemed disinterested in them and in a rush to get off the phone to get dinner, now has a dozen questions. The girl tells him about how she had a cut and the mother left a bandage on her leg for three days, forgetting to change it or check it, and about how when the mother did pull the bandage off, finally, beneath were two large mounds full of pus. Then the next day, there were several more pustules on the girl's leg. Hence the antibiotic delivered in a supply box.

The husband says, "Did you not bathe her for three whole days?"

The mother says, "I forgot. And it's not like she gets dirty never leaving the house. I'm just trying to survive. It's not easy doing everything myself."

He says, "Well, I hope our daughter survives, too."

The mother says nothing.

After they say their goodbyes and hang up the phone, the girl says, "I wish I had gotten to see the rabbit head. I wish you had called me."

"That would be breaking protocol now, wouldn't it?" the mother says.

"I never get to see anything," the girl says.

Of course, the mother longs for the girl to grow up differently. She longs for the girl to be safe in the outside world, to roam free. But absolutely she must ensure that the girl follows protocol. Absolutely she must keep the girl safe.

*

In 1903, a neurologist named Sir Henry Head elected to sever the radial nerve in his left arm for science. He knew that people who experience nerve damage regain sensation over time, and he wanted to map this recovery. What sensations returned first? Second? He and a co-experimenter subjected his left arm to all manner of stimulations over a period of about five years.

If the mother knew about Sir Henry Head's experiment, she would likely say that pregnancy and giving birth had been like severing an important nerve. Seven years later, the mother is still recovering what she lost, only the difference is her experiment is not controlled. There is no mirrored half, like Head's right arm, that preserves her pre-pregnant self.

That she chose to get pregnant, wanted a child, despite all the facts, despite having observed her mother in the situation she is in now is a testament to the power of hormones, the mother supposes. Hormones make you do things that are not in your best interest. Hormones are not to be trusted. The problem is you can never be certain when your desires and behaviors are ruled by hormones and when they are not. Perhaps when she wishes the husband were dead, that is hormones. Perhaps the moments she feels tender toward him are the products of hormones. Perhaps when the mother stands at the window and watches the neighbor woman walk out of her house in T-shirt and shorts and sneakers and take off running down the street, no apparent worries about being a woman alone on a street, and the mother longs to abandon the girl and run out after the woman, that is hormones. Perhaps remaining at the window instead of joining the woman is hormones.

*

Although she is not allowed to leave the house, the mother is allowed to blog. In fact, blogging is encouraged. A routine is good, having some sort of work besides cleaning house and rearing a child is good, the husband has said.

The mother is a baker blogger. If you are a baker blogger, you are, de facto, a memoirist. Each new recipe comes wrapped in anecdotes from your life.

There is much the mother cannot share on her blog, of course. Like that the husband is away a lot. Because what if among her readers is a man who sees an opportunity? A mother and child alone. This concern was suggested by the husband, but she shares the same worry, though she'd never admit it to him. His absence makes her nervous, especially at night when she can't see more than a few feet out the house's windows. They have a treadmill in their garage, and often when the girl is in bed at night, the mother considers going out there and running on it, but the garage, though an extension of the house, feels separate from the house.

She worries that somehow she'd get locked out there, separated from the girl, and that something terrible would happen.

There is plenty she enjoys about the husband's absence too. That their bathroom is all hers, for instance. No husband bending over the sink to brush his teeth, a mix of toothpaste and saliva dribbling down his chin into the basin. No mysterious wads of toilet paper on the floor next to the trash bin. No stubble hairs on her bar of soap. But these details she cannot share on the blog either, for they would embarrass the husband, hurt his feelings.

She does not dare post stories about the girl, either, for there are men who will masturbate to these stories.

So the mother has invented a persona for her blog. The baker of her blog is childless and single. This isn't simply an act of omission: because she does not mention the girl or the husband, ergo, they do not exist. No, the baker in the blog tells her readers she is too selfish to have children, too particular and too hermit-prone to marry. She posts photographs of gorgeous cakes and cookies and writes about how nothing else in life fulfills her the way baking does.

When the mother began the blog, she thought she would blog once a week on Tuesdays. But, quickly, baking and blogging about baking became a necessity. Now she bakes and blogs almost daily. If she can't bake during the day, say the girl is sick, and she must lie next to the girl to keep her company, then she bakes at night when the girl is passed out from a heavy dose of alcohol-laden cough syrup.

They throw a lot of baked goods into the garbage chute.

The mother thinks often of that fairy tale, "Sweet Porridge," about a poor woman and her child who live alone. They have nothing to eat until the child goes into the forest and an old woman gives her a magic pot. When the girl says, "Little pot, cook," the pot makes sweet porridge. When she says, "Little pot, stop," the pot stops. One day while the girl is away, the mother commands the pot to cook and it does, only the mother does not know the command to make it stop. So the pot cooks and cooks until the whole town is buried in porridge. Does the mother drown in all this porridge? The story does not say.

*

As the girl steps out of the bath and the mother presses a towel to the girl's wet hair, the girl says, "I want to slice you open and wear your skin like a house."

The mother plays a game with the girl sometimes, a game she learned from her own mother, in which they use a house as a metaphor for everything and anything that contains, as in a sock is a house for a foot, a lock is a house for a key, a mouth is a house for teeth.

The girl leans into the mother the way she always does after a bath, wraps her wet limbs around the mother. She is so small, so easy to break, and the outside is full of men who wish to break her. Is it any wonder the girl should want to hide in her mother's skin?

The mother worries about the girl's fear. The girl has never played with another child. She has never seen another child except on television or in books. The girl will not know how to be with other people. She will be afraid, suspicious, awkward.

The mother often watches the neighbor—pruning her roses or backing out of the driveway in a car, sunglasses concealing her eyes. The mother once did these things before she got pregnant. She could have chosen to remain unpregnant, un-mothered, free. She was never comfortable in the world, though. She wonders if this has much to do with why she became pregnant. Maybe it was less hormones, more fear.

What she couldn't have known was that there is plenty to fear in here too. All mothers must fear at some point that their children may hurt them. That's putting it too mildly. All children *do* hurt their mothers. They tear their way out of their mother's bodies, after all, unless a doctor cuts into the mother instead of the child's head and shoulders. And then there is the biting of her nipples, the exhaustion when the child cries in the middle of the night, the first time the child hits the mother, the first time the child says to the mother that she hates her or that the mother is stupid or ugly or unlovable. Such injuries are accepted as normal. Children separating their identities from that of the mother, psychologists say, may be cruel. It's a necessary violence.

The mother, being a woman, has come to expect a certain level of cruelty and violence. Like outside, when men on the street have yelled at her, before she got pregnant and left the outside, that she looked like she needed to be fucked. Or when a man on the street grabbed her ass. Or when a man in the office she used to work in would talk

197

over her again and again in meetings. Or when the husband, before he became the husband, told her no one else would ever love her like he loves her. A declaration he seemed to think should make her feel loved, but what she heard was that she ought to feel lucky he bothers with her because nobody else would.

Still, there are many moments with the girl when the mother wonders: is this something she should heed? Like when the girl found a small lizard in the house and she made a "leash" for the animal with some yarn and tied it to the coffee table, and the lizard promptly strangled itself.

There are many other moments, having nothing to do with the girl presumably, which also prompt the mother to wonder if she should take heed. The decapitated rabbit head, for instance. The mother must make a choice in these moments: either she takes heed and is afraid and, more often than not, her husband dismisses her fear; or she does not take heed and risks being guilty of being heedless.

*

The next time the mother hears the thunk of the supply box, she looks out the peephole half-expecting to find another decapitated rabbit head, but instead there is something a bit larger, rounder, something she can't quite make out through the fisheye lens. Dog shit perhaps.

Protocol does not include anything about unidentifiable-from-the-peephole objects accompanying a supply box.

She takes a breath and opens the door. She sees that the object she couldn't identify through the peephole is a rattlesnake, coiled against the side of the box.

Protocol entails that the mother quickly open the door, quickly drag the supply box into the house, and quickly shut the door. Protocol does not include anything about rattlesnakes.

The mother knows rattlesnakes are not eager to strike, that they do so only when startled or threatened. But quickly dragging the box will surely startle or threaten the rattlesnake.

She shuts the door. She counts to three. She looks out the peephole. The snake is still there.

Perhaps if she drags the box slowly, slowly, the snake will not startle or feel threatened? She could hook the top of the box with the rake from the garage. She could wear boots as she does this. She could wrap leftover scraps of carpet around her legs with duct tape. Perhaps the thickness of the carpet will be enough to prevent the snake's fangs from reaching her skin.

The girl is watching television. She is so entranced that she pays no attention to the mother going in and out of the garage, the noise of the duct tape.

When the mother is finally ready about fifteen minutes later, she opens the door.

The snake is gone.

The mother throws stale macaroons around the box to be sure. No movement. No sounds aside from the thunks of the macaroons.

The mother puts down the rake and quickly drags in the supply box. She quickly shuts the door.

She worries she imagined the snake. She worries about the break in protocol. She worries the snake is real and one among many creatures trying to get inside the house.

She thinks of the tree outside her bedroom. Years ago when it was a much smaller tree she and the husband brought home from the nursery in a black plastic pot, like a diaper the way the pot held the soil around the tree's roots, she planted the tree closer to the house than she ought to have. She didn't understand then about roots, how far they spread, the damage they can do. She imagines the tree's roots pushing up against the house's foundation, cracking the foundation like cracking an egg into a bowl. Sometimes late at night, when the house is otherwise quiet, she thinks she hears the tree's roots pawing beneath the house.

*

In the fairy tales the mother reads the girl before bed, the monsters are often mothers. Stepmothers, birth mothers, old hags—same difference.

In the horror films the mother watches some evenings when the girl is asleep, the monsters are often children. Adopted children, biological children, little men who are mistaken for children.

The girl is often startling the mother—at night when she wakes from a nightmare and walks into the kitchen while the mother is baking, in the mornings when the mother is drinking coffee and doesn't realize the girl is up. The girl treads silently. No warning. Or like now, the mother walks right by the girl where the girl is curled up on the sofa, and the mother doesn't see the girl until the girl speaks. The mother screams.

After the girl stops crying, she says, "Why did you scream?"

The mother says, "I thought I was alone."

The girl looks confused and also frightened. "Why would you think that?"

*

The husband calls while the mother is licking a thin frosting from her fingers. A boiled orange cake is baking in the oven.

The girl is in a television trance. The mother thinks that perhaps the television has sucked the girl out of her body, that the girl's body is an empty husk, the way she sits so still, eyes fixed. A television is a house for a girl, she thinks. But then the girl laughs at something on the screen, and the mother is assured the girl is still in there somewhere.

Instead of immediately giving the phone to the girl as she often does, the mother tells the husband about the rattlesnake and about what the girl said about wanting to slit her open and wear her skin.

The husband says, "She says funny stuff, doesn't she? Have you followed protocol?"

The mother says, "I couldn't follow protocol precisely when the rattlesnake was next to the supply box. I had to close the door and come up with a plan for how to get the box. So I had to open the door twice that morning. I had to let the box sit for a bit outside."

The husband says, "Hmm. Probably everything is OK."

The mother says, "What could I have done differently? Offered a leg for the snake to bite?"

The husband says, "Nothing like this all these years and then a rabbit head and then a snake. It doesn't seem possible."

The mother says, "Are you calling me crazy?"

"I'm saying it's probably nothing. There's nothing to worry about."

"It's been five weeks now. When are you coming home?"

The husband says, "You know I don't know. And even if I did, I couldn't tell you."

The mother says, "I don't want to live like this anymore."

"What does that mean?"

"I might as well not even have a husband."

The husband says, "Well, maybe I'll die on the job, and you won't have a husband anymore. And then you'll get a fat insurance check. Won't that be nice?" The husband laughs.

*

There are three types of baker bloggers. First, there are the bakers who invent. They create brand new sweets the world has never tasted before. Or they reinvent classics, making them truly their own—revamped recipes you could not possibly confuse with the originals. This group of baker bloggers is the rarest. Second, there are the bakers who purport to be inventors, who present recipes as their own despite that said recipes are entirely generic. They get away with it perhaps because their readers aren't concerned with originality. They just want a good recipe made easily reproducible by beautiful photos and clear instructions. This is the most common group of baker bloggers. The mother is neither of these types. She is the third type, the baker who bakes other people's recipes, classic recipes, without pretending she has made them her own.

The mother would like to invent recipes of her own, but she doesn't feel ready yet. There is still so much she hasn't made. There is still so much to learn. The idea of wasting ingredients on failures causes her stress. Worse: What if she were to present to the world something as her own that is not?

Someone with the username BlackEyedSue comments on the mother's blog one evening: "Why do you only ever bake other people's recipes?"

The mother writes back, "I'm apprenticing."

BlackEyedSue writes, "This blog is six years old."

*

The husband has been gone 39 days when the girl says, "I want to die."

When the mother asks her why, the girl says, "Because I'm a horrible, horrible girl."

The mother is quiet. She thinks of the lizard. She thinks of her own flesh sliced open like a baked potato. Then she says, "You are a wonderful girl. And nobody is perfect. We all do things we're ashamed of. Did you do something you're ashamed of?"

The girl repeats, "I want to die." Then she says, "I want everyone to die. I want the whole world to die."

The mother feels sad and scared and, strangely, the tiniest bit proud. The girl has always been a smart, sensitive child. The mother has always taught the girl to express her emotions. And who hasn't felt this way at some time or another?

On the other hand, is this one of those moments in which she ought to take heed?

She worries about her culpability. She loves the girl, but she has never enjoyed playing with her. Playing with the girl is, in fact, almost the worst way to spend her time that she can imagine. When the husband is home, she'll say to him, you play with our daughter, and I'll do these dishes. The husband thinks he is getting the better deal, the mother thinks she is getting the better deal.

At night when the mother takes the girl to bed, the girl clings to the mother like she's all that's keeping the girl from falling from a steep cliff. Perhaps the girl does not feel secure. Because the mother so clearly prefers baking and chores to playing with the girl.

When the mother does spend time with the girl, it is usually to watch movies, and usually she has wine in hand because the movies her daughter enjoys are mostly boring or even if they're not boring, the mother has watched them with the girl five times already.

Also, the mother frequently zones out while the girl is talking. Sometimes the girl catches her. "Mama, did you hear what I said?"

Just that morning, this had happened. Instead of listening to her child, the mother had been thinking about how she misses orgasms. She is perfectly good at delivering them herself, sans the husband. The problem is the girl is in her bed every night now. She won't even start the night in her own bed. The mother could take a vibrator to her child's bedroom or the hall bathroom, lock the door and be done within a few minutes, but the idea of masturbating in either of these locations is wholly unappealing. The most appealing location for masturbation, other than in the privacy of her own bedroom, is the sofa under a throw while she reads a book or watches television. But there's no way to lock her bedroom from the outside to ensure the girl does not come out.

The mother says, "Well, I certainly hope you don't die any time soon."

This is true, but the mother considers that there would be some consolation in being able to leave the house, in being able to mourn outside in the sunshine and the fresh air.

*

That evening while the girl is in the bath, the mother stands at the window and watches the woman next door throw a stick across her lawn to a small, brown dog. The mother has never seen the dog before. The woman must have brought it home that very day. The mother thinks of the woman driving to a shelter, walking from her car to the shelter, choosing whatever dog she wants.

The dog fetches the stick, but the dog does not bring the stick back to the woman. The dog has not yet learned this game. The woman has to run after the dog and take the stick from its mouth. She throws the stick again. She calls to the dog. The mother hears the woman calling, "Muffin! Muffin!"

The mother taps the glass then. She imagines her and the woman smiling and waving at each other, but the woman does not turn. The mother taps harder. The woman does not turn.

Then the girl taps the mother's hip, and the mother startles. She falls backward into the console table next to the window. Her thigh strikes the corner of the table, forming a bruise that turns blue-black by morning.

*

There is no more sugar or wine in the cupboard. No more eggs in the refrigerator. The stock of toilet paper, dish soap, coffee, yogurt, chicken stock, oatmeal, hand cream, frozen mangos, coconut oil, waxing strips, and sea salt truffles is low. Although supply boxes are easy to order and always arrive promptly, the mother has never before allowed her stocks to get so low before ordering reinforcements. Some part of her has never fully trusted that she'd be able to get what she needed when she needed it. And with the husband away and impossible to contact, what would she do if a box didn't arrive?

There is a grocery store barely two miles away. The woman next door shops there. The mother knows because sometimes the woman forgets her cloth bags and removes from the trunk of her car paper bags bearing the store's name.

The mother no longer owns a car. If there were an emergency that required immediate medical care, they would call paramedics. If necessary, the paramedics would take the mother and the girl to the hospital. There is a phone number engraved into a locket hanging from the mother's neck. Even if the mother were unconscious, the paramedics would open the locket and call the number. It is an emergency number to be used only in an emergency. A stranger, not the husband, would answer and would notify the husband immediately, at which point he would either return immediately or make some other preparations to make sure the mother and the girl are looked after, kept safe.

Running out of food and no supply box arriving: would that constitute an emergency, when a grocery store is just a couple miles away?

As she makes a list of the items they need, she pictures the rabbit head; the rattlesnake; tree roots like fingers scratching underneath their house, poking at the foundation.

The scariest movie the mother ever saw was Hitchcock's *The Birds*. What made it so scary was its lack of explanation for why the birds attacked.

*

When the husband calls, she does not tell him about the girl's latest talk of killing her, and the entire human population. She hands the phone to the girl.

While the girl talks to the husband, the mother studies her list. Should she order pistachios and finally tackle a baked Alaska, the dessert she's been most intimidated by all these years? The one that she'd told herself would be the finale end of her apprenticeship? Because if she could manage to seal in the semifreddo with a sturdy barrier of meringue and torch the ice-cream cake without creating an oozing mess, she could do anything, couldn't she?

She hears the girl say, "I didn't see the snake." Then, "She was banging on the window last night."

The mother takes the phone from the girl. "What are you doing?" she says to the husband.

"I just asked her if you guys had seen any more rattlesnakes," he says. "I just wanted to know how you two are doing, just making sure you're both OK."

"Just," she says. Then the mother tells him about how the other day the girl said she wanted the mother to die.

The girl looks at her feet.

"Children don't have much of a filter," the husband says. "I bet you've wished sometimes I'm dead. You just don't say it. Oh, wait: You have."

The mother says, "I never said that."

"Perhaps not so directly."

"She said she wished everybody in the whole world was dead."

The girl starts crying.

"Angela," he says. "She's six." Then, "I can't make any promises, as you know, but there's a good chance I may be home within the week. Maybe much sooner. I can't say for sure, though, as you know."

She says nothing.

"Did you hear me?"

She hangs up the phone, turns off the ringer.

She puts her arm around the girl, says to her, "Everything's OK." She gives the girl one of the giant almond horn cookies with sprinkles she'd made the day before. Then while the girl watches television, the mother eats three.

*

She puts in her order for a supply box, schedules it for dusk because she has never scheduled a supply box for dusk and so she surmises that whoever or whatever is menacing her will be caught off guard.

Twenty minutes before the box is to arrive, the mother paces near the front window. She watches the woman next door pull into her driveway. Another car pulls in behind her car. A man steps out. He is tall and handsome and wearing a forest green pullover sweater. The husband owns a sweater much like it, only his is more blue. Or maybe not. The more she considers the color of that sweater, the less sure she is of the color.

The mother thinks it can't be cold enough out to warrant a sweater, not when so few of the leaves have fallen from the trees. This makes her think she doesn't like this man. The way the man stands there waiting for the woman to walk to him bothers her too. Even the way he puts his hand on her arm, like he's laying claim.

The mother watches them disappear into the house.

Five minutes before the box is to arrive, the mother leans over the back of the sofa to kiss the top of the girl's head. The girl smells like popcorn.

When the mother hears the thunk of the supply box, she is in position. She takes a deep breath. She leans into the peephole.

She almost makes a sound but quickly covers her mouth. There is a man at her door or at least she thinks the figure is a man. She neglected to turn on the porchlight, and it's just dark enough out now that the figure is more silhouette than flesh. His feet blend in with the supply box, so that his calves appear rooted.

The lights are off on the inside of the house as well, so she knows that even if he could see more than her eyeball through the opposite end of the fisheye lens, all he could possibly see now is blackness.

She breathes quietly. Watches the figure lean in too, until he is so close that his head blocks out the faint traces of sunlight.

Is he pressing himself against the door?

She places her palm against the door, then her entire body. She wonders if she might feel the figure's breath and his blood pumping if she listens with her whole body.

When the knock comes, it reverberates through her bones. A code she tries to decipher.

The knock seems to emerge at the small of her back, to thrum there.

Another knock. Only this time the knocking seems to be coming from both the door and from behind her.

She realizes that what she feels at the small of her back is not the knock that moves through the door and into her bones, but a finger. The girl's finger.

"It's me," a voice whispers, but whether it comes from the outside or from the inside, she isn't sure.

The mother stiffens. If she stands very still, maybe no one will know she is there.

"A Mouth is a House for Teeth" originally appeared in *Colorado Review*.

Paper Cut

by Clare Weze

They asked me to make a man for Aunty Heidi, so that's what I did.

It didn't take me long. I decided to do her a man in black, because then he'd be eye-catching and sophisticated and I could give his jacket straight, square shoulders. I drew him on cardboard and cut him out in seconds. Modelling clay would have been too heavy, and I had a feeling she wanted someone bendy. I stuck a paper face on, coloured his hair in black felt pen, and gave him long, delicate paper hands.

One thing bugged me: his hair looked like felt pen. I ran to the beach and found the perfect material straight away: seaweed. Black, washed up that morning, and all dried out. Back at home, I snipped it into short strands and glued it on. Now his hair looked like it was flowing, even growing, as if he'd just washed it. I sniffed. Yes, you could still smell seaweed, but it was fresh. I took him round to her flat just as the sun was sitting perfectly on the watery horizon across the bay. A Morecambe man made with real Morecambe seaweed.

"He's magnificent!" she said. "Just what I need. Thank you, Natalie."

"Why do you need a man, Aunty Heidi?" Mum had said it was because she was lonely, but I didn't believe that; she's always had loads of friends. There was some kind of tangle between Mum and Aunty Heidi. They hadn't quite fallen out, but they weren't exactly huggy sisters any more.

"I need someone to mend my washing machine," she said. "And shave a fraction off the bottom of my front door to stop it sticking."

"Dad can do that."

"Hmm. I think I need to stop bothering your dad."

My cardboard man sat in Aunty Heidi's palms, his white face cradled against her thumb, his fingers spread delicately, as if he was just about to play the piano. They didn't look like strong, mending fingers. "Can't you just phone the washing machine shop?"

She didn't answer. She studied the man in her hands as if she, too, was wondering what he could do. Then she propped him between her teacup and a jar of honey, buttered our toast, as usual, and asked me about my day.

Our house is next door to Aunty Heidi's, so when she went out the next day wearing a pale green dress I'd never seen before, with her hair up in a clip, I jumped down from the window and raced after her.

She was quite a way ahead of me, so I shouted her name, but my voice was drowned out by a motorbike. I didn't shout again. I followed her all the way to the Midland Hotel, which is as far as I'm allowed.

She went inside, which was so weird. Aunty Heidi always tells me if she's going somewhere special. I watched her disappear through the big glass doors, then ran up to them and peered through. There she was, waiting in the middle of the floor beneath the circular staircase. There were lots of people; my ears rang with the buzz of their chatter. Then a man came up to her. I didn't see where he came from; he was just suddenly there, jangling keys in his pockets as he walked. Aunty Heidi turned to him and they held hands for a second. Blink and you'd have missed it. He was dressed in black, like my cardboard man. Black trousers, black shirt, black shoes … and dark hair.

They went to the Rotunda Bar. I followed. They sat near the window, with drinks. I stood in the doorway near the top of the basement stairs and looked into the amazing round room with its glass wall, like the one in Aunty Heidi's flat, and its chandelier. Aunty Heidi has one of those, too. The whole hotel could almost BE Aunty Heidi's flat, but about a hundred times bigger.

Aunty Heidi looked excited. She smiled a lot more than usual. She talked, and smiled as she talked, showing her teeth. What could they be saying? She looked a bit stiff, as if she was doing something difficult. Then he went back to the bar for more drinks and I got a better view of him: he was young, tall and thin with a pale face, just like the man

I'd made. Perhaps if he'd been wearing jeans, or if he hadn't been so tall … but no, he was dressed exactly as I'd made him.

He sat down again and this time, he was leaning right over Aunty Heidi and all I could see of her was a little sprig of red hair poking out from behind his black head. He must have bewitched her. What can you talk about that's so important you have to get close up like that? And if my cardboard man had come to life, then he probably DID have strange powers. Should I rescue her? Should I walk across to them and pretend Mum wanted her for something?

I tried to make out the strands of seaweed-hair. If I did walk up to them, I'd be able to see the seaweed. I'd be able to touch it. I'd know.

*

I couldn't do it. Outside, the traffic crawled along both lanes beside me. I scanned the sea. The tide was miles away. I ran along the prom towards home, but I didn't really want to go there. My best friend Megan was away in Greece all summer, otherwise I'd have been straight round to her house.

At home, Mum was on the computer, but I didn't let that stop me. "Mum! Aunty Heidi's with a man in the Midland Hotel!"

"What? How do you know?"

"I've seen her. And he's dangerous! He's not a real man! He's a *thing*!"

"What do you mean? Anyway, it's none of our business who Aunty Heidi sees. Don't be nosy."

"No, it's that man I made for her—you know, The Man! He's come to life!"

But of course, Mum just laughed. "Tell 'em tall, tell 'em all, tell 'em to the wall."

*

When Aunty Heidi came home from work the next day, I was waiting on her doorstep. I asked her about the man all the way up the stairs. "I saw you through the window in the Midland. He's your boyfriend, isn't he? Why didn't you tell me you had a boyfriend?"

She shook her head and laughed. "DREAM A LITTLE DREAM OF ME," she sang from her bedroom as she swapped her white dental nurse's uniform for a summer dress.

I shouted through, "Where did you find him?"

"We just got talking and we clicked."

"But where?" I could hear her getting cross with the tangle of coat hangers in her wardrobe.

"Here, there, everywhere," she said, coming back to sit with me. "Just around. All around the place."

"But that's like when I ask how old you are and you say, 'As old as my tongue and a little bit older than my teeth.'"

Aunty Heidi giggled. "And that's true too! It's the God's honest truth. No, really, I met him on the Lunesdale Studio Trail. I've signed up for a course in mosaics. He's a sculptor, and he's going to make a seahorse for my windowsill."

I studied her face. People's eyes try to concentrate on something when they're lying, but her eyes just looked into mine and crinkled when she smiled, so I wasn't sure. Because just lately, Mum says Aunty Heidi makes it up as she goes along.

I thought of something. "Where's The Man?"

"What man?"

"The MAN. The man I made you."

"Oh. He's on the bookcase, I think." She got up and went over to look. "Perhaps not."

"Have you lost him?"

"Course not, Sweetheart. I treasure the things you make me. He's probably in the bedroom."

There wasn't anything suspicious in her voice or the way she looked, but I didn't believe her—not one word. "I'll try to find him for you," I said, and I wandered from room to room, feeling a little bit spooked, as if secretly, The Man was here, playing a game with me.

I like Aunty Heidi's flat; it's much tidier than our house, and calmer too. There's only Aunty Heidi living there, for one thing, and for another, whatever Aunty Heidi does in her place, Mum does the opposite in ours. I couldn't find The Man.

Back at home, I pushed my food all around my plate instead of eating.

"The man I made her isn't there any more," I said, "and that man she met in the Midland is pretending to be a sculptor. He's tricking her. He's probably pretending he can help with her mosaic classes."

Mum looked up from her dinner. "Mosaic classes? Since when did she decide to do mosaics?"

"I don't know. She's even told him that seahorses are her favourite creatures."

Mum put her knife and fork down. "I thought we were both going to do watercolours. That's what she said."

"She met him at the Lunesdale Trail. It must be a walk through a wood."

"No, it's an art thing, so he could be anyone—a visitor, perhaps. But that doesn't mean he's tricking her, Natalie. You're getting carried away." She picked up her cup of tea and cradled it next to her mouth without drinking. "Well, he'll know he's got her, that's for sure. What's his name, anyway?"

I gasped. "She never said!"

I BET HE HASN'T GOT ONE! I remembered how small and neat he'd looked in her hand when he was still cardboard. TEENSY. HARMLESS-LOOKING. But the most deadly octopus is only the size of a marble. Aunty Heidi told me that.

Dad was already clearing the dishes away, saying nothing. I could tell he was listening, though. His shoulders were stiff, and he looked over at Mum every few seconds.

I made plans. I'd follow The Man and find out where he slept, see if he turned back into cardboard when people weren't looking. I clicked through the internet, looking for things that change. BUTTERFLIES ... FROGS ... Wherever I clicked, I found METAMORPHOSIS, but nothing quite like The Man. I landed on a page with a beautiful picture of a dragonfly and remembered what Aunty Heidi once told me about them: they live for two years as a nymph underwater, then spend just one month as an adult above ground. Like The Man, perhaps? Just a month would be okay.

All that week I looked out for him. On the beach, all around the new flats, at the fairground. But I never found him on his own. No matter how I timed it, he always got to Aunty Heidi's flat without me seeing.

One day, after I'd given up trying to beat him, I decided to follow the pair of them again. At first it went well. They didn't look back, so I got brave and by the time they'd reached the play area I was just behind them. This was the closest I'd ever been and I could smell him. He smelt of cooking oil and Mars bars. I had to get even closer to hear what they were saying.

"And the devil take the hindmost," Aunty Heidi said.

"Do you get me?" he said. His voice was low and croaky, like a crow.

I missed her answer to that, but next, she said, "As long as nothing crops up."

"That was real," he said.

What was real? I couldn't understand them. His hair looked as if he'd polished it.

Then Aunty Heidi stopped and they both turned around suddenly. "Natalie!"

I jumped.

"Rod and I are just going for a little walk by ourselves."

ROD? Huh! And what on Earth did they talk about all the time? He wouldn't know about any of the things Aunty Heidi liked to tell me—the dragonfly nymphs, the moons of Jupiter, how nettles sting you with tiny injection needles.

He could only possibly be interested in greasy things. I could tell by the way he smelled.

*

I didn't think Aunty Heidi would ever forget me. Mum and Dad go to see a film at the Dukes cinema once a month and drop me at ballet first. Aunty Heidi always picks me up, takes me home, and stays with me till they get back, as it's late and the house is empty. Or sometimes we watch a film at her place. But that one night, she was too busy doing whatever it was she did with The Man, and I came out of ballet and waited next to the sweet shop … and waited. Mum and Dad turn their mobiles off in the Dukes. Aunty Heidi wasn't answering hers.

It's a long way back from Bare. Too long. At first it was like an adventure, as if the whole of Morecambe had been laid out for me to explore. But that feeling didn't last long. There weren't many people on Seaborn Grove, which made me feel like everyone knew a better way and was taking it.

I felt loose, like a boat cast adrift. I headed for the sea. There was Marine Road. There was the beach, the sea, the big rocks with perching stone seagulls. The real seagulls hunched their wings against the wind. My coat blew forward and my hair flew high in the air, knotting up and stinging my eyes, so by the time I got home I looked icky and messed up and my lips tasted salty. Even the sea looked sulky and grey. The tide was in and the waves slumped against the concrete wall as if they wanted to slap somebody.

I reached the house at the same time as Mum and Dad, which was wrong, wrong, wrong.

"Where've you been?" said Mum. "Where's Heidi?"

"She never turned up. She's probably with that man." I glanced up at the dark windows of Aunty Heidi's flat.

"What?" Mum yanked the door open and tugged her jacket off. "She's left you to walk home on your own?"

We all stood in the kitchen. They stared at me.

"Are you all right?" asked Dad.

I nodded.

"Is that bloke leading her by the nose, or what?" said Mum.

We heard the click of Aunty Heidi's garden gate, and a giggle.

"Right," said Mum. She says that just before she does something important. RIGHT.

A horrible hot feeling swept through me. "What are you going to do? She just forgot."

"June," Dad said. "You'll regret it. You know you will."

But Mum left the house.

"What will she regret?" I asked, but Dad just shook his head and gave me the lot-of-fuss-about-nothing look, which I might have believed if his eyebrows hadn't given him away. They go up into little arrowheads when he's worried. I found a pen and drew loose eyebrows on his newspaper till Mum came back.

She made cheese on toast for supper. Dad stood back and let her do it. He didn't ask. I made an arrowhead out of my knife and fork, carefully, without wobbling the table.

Mum and Aunty Heidi. The gap between them went on for weeks. And nearly every day The Man slipped up the stairs next door. You only ever caught a glimpse of him—his back disappearing, or sometimes a side view—but always, a feeling came off him, a kind of gloating. I think he was glad about the argument because now he could have Aunty Heidi all to himself. I even saw him in the morning, once. The week before term started again, I looked up at her window on my way to feed Megan's rabbits and there he stood, his dark head filling the pane. He yawned when he saw me, as if he'd just woken up. It was the most awful yawn I've ever seen in my life. It went on for ages and was wider than a mouth should really be.

"Can we go bowling?" I asked Mum one day.

"I've got a lot to do. Maybe later."

"You're all busy. Megan's on holiday, and Aunty Heidi's with that man."

"Don't bother your aunt."

"It's not like a summer holiday," I said. A seagull squawked outside our window.

Mum took hold of my cheeks in both hands and squeezed. "That's the way it goes sometimes." She looked dreamy. "Why don't you go to the beach or play around the fountains? If you wait for other people to make your entertainment, you'll be waiting and waiting till Christmas has been and gone." I had the feeling she wasn't just talking about me.

I dreamt about how easy it would be to get rid of him. I could just throw him in the sea and watch him soak and float. In a while, he'd disintegrate and get washed up with the line of froth. Or I could walk across the sands when the tide was out and bury him. Aunty Heidi's told me there are fields of gas under that sea. If I walked far enough out and dug far enough down, I could bury him on top of the sandstone where the gas is stored. I liked the idea of him being on top of a load of gas. Or I could just cut him into little ribbons and throw him in the bin. The only trouble was, I couldn't find him, could I? Not in his true cardboard form, anyway.

Then I had my brainwave: CARDBOARD. Wouldn't a cardboard man be happier with a cardboard woman?

I got my scissors out again. I made her blonde and as pretty as I could, which was easy because I've got lots of Clarice Bean books and there are some lovely faces to copy in those. I made her dress out of actual red velvet from an old cushion and stuck it on with super-glue. Her shoes were real Cinderella slippers made from a shiny blue plastic bag with mega-high heels. I got really into it. The heels were cut from a white yoghurt pot; I thought I'd better make them fairly sturdy.

I took her round to Aunty Heidi's with some biscuits I'd made. "Has it come to this, Petal?" Dad teased, but I was glad. The biscuits would get me in—me and the cardboard woman.

"Back to school soon," said Aunty Heidi.

The Man didn't speak at all, and he ate none of my biscuits. I glared at him. DRAGONFLY, I thought.

"You'll be glad to see Megan again." Aunty Heidi rubbed her hands together and cleared our cups and plates away. She looked as if she was in a hurry to wash up.

I hid the cardboard woman in the bathroom window behind a spare loo roll. And it was odd, because as soon as I'd put her in position, one of those thin spindly spiders began to spin round and round on its web in a corner near the ceiling. They don't usually do that unless you touch them.

It didn't take long. I saw the two of them together—the cardboard man and the cardboard lady—in that café in front of the Battery just three days later on a rainy teatime. Her glass slippers looked solid enough now.

"Four chocolate chip cookies to take away, please," I said at the counter. I was sure The Man would look across when he heard my voice, but he didn't. Perhaps he was just pretending not to listen. Outside, seagulls screeched and swooped over the wet sand. After walking a little way, I looked back over my shoulder and thought I saw them both staring after me.

*

"Told you he'd be a fly-by-night," said Mum, when we found out Aunty Heidi was on her own again.

"When did you say that?" I asked, but neither Mum nor Dad wanted to talk about Aunty Heidi or her ex-man. They did have her to tea, though, for the first time in months.

Mum grumbled about the only type of bread that had been left in Tesco's, and then raved about the cakes in the

Italian market ("They're magnificent!") and the rice at the new Nepalese stall ("You have to watch them or they persuade you into all kinds."). But I could tell she was trying her best.

Aunty Heidi was wary, but agreed as hard as she could. "You have to stop them piling chutney into the small tubs and squashing it down. Before you know it, you've parted with ten pounds."

Nobody mentioned The Man, but everyone was thinking about him, and it felt like it might start raining on us any second, even though we were in the kitchen.

"We could go bowling again now," I said to Aunty Heidi.

She looked down at her hands for a moment. "That would be fun, Natalie."

"You'll get all the strikes," I told her, to cheer her up, and she smiled at me but her eyes stayed sad and sort of worn out.

I'd been back at school for nearly a month before she started laughing properly again and taking me to places, showing me things like she used to. She wasn't fuzzy and dreamy any more, but she wasn't quite the same as she'd been before I made that man, either. Never quite the same again.

"Paper Cut" originally appeared in *Cloudscapes Over the Lune*.

Dandelion

by Olga Zilberbourg

A story Oz had written nearly won a prize. Though the story came in second, it received some notice. A New York agent contacted her. "I have read the story of yours and think it's wonderful. Do you have a novel you need representation for?"

Oz had no novel, but she did have a nineteen month-old. "He's very much like a novel," she told the agent. "Can I ship him to you? People are telling me that, since he can walk, he's no longer a baby. Soon, he'll be ready for publication."

The agent asked to see a picture. Oz sent a recent image of the child in the park, holding a white-headed dandelion by the stem. The child's pale curls, backlit by the setting sun, resembled the dandelion.

The agent liked the picture and asked to see "Dandelion" in person.

Before shipping her child off to New York, Oz added the final touches. She cut his hair and trimmed his nails. She gave him a long bath, to scrub the dandruff from his scalp and the playground grime from his feet. She outfitted him with a leash harness, so he wouldn't be able to run into traffic. She cut off feet from his pajamas and straps from his hat to make it look more like a baseball cap. She taught him to smile and give high-fives when he was too shy to say "Hello." Oz didn't have time to teach him to use the toilet, and this concerned her a great deal. She wrote to the agent, asking for advice, but the agent assured her it would be fine. If a publisher would take "Dandelion" on, they would toilet-train using their preferred method. "I frequently advise authors to leave one obvious flaw for the publisher to edit," the agent wrote. "The editors will edit, and unless you give them something obvious to work with, they are liable to start messing with the parts they better leave alone."

Having done everything she could think of, Oz presented the child to her husband. Her husband was Oz's first reader, and though not very familiar with the publishing industry, gave common sense advice that helped her make sure she was on the right track. "You may have cut his hair too short," the husband said, running his fingers across the child's head. "Otherwise, he's perfect." He asked the child to point out his belly button and then tickled him until the child was squealing with laughter. "I'm going to miss him," the husband said. "But, I guess, if he's to be published, I'll see him soon."

The husband helped Oz to package and ship "Dandelion" to New York.

Then, they waited.

The agent acknowledged the receipt, and said that "Dandelion" was just as beautiful in person as he'd looked in the picture.

A week later, she wrote to say that he was a very active child with boundless curiosity, and that she would right away introduce him to several publishers and schedule an auction. She asked if there were a code word or a particular bedtime routine that could help "Dandelion" relax and be still for more than a few minutes at a time. Reading books to him didn't seem to help; he wanted to flip the pages himself and kept asking to see the cats. "I'm not sure what cats he means. These old school publishers are tired," she wrote. "They want to take on familiar, well-behaved projects."

Oz suggested taking "Dandelion" on a good long walk, to tire him out, and then giving him a bath.

When she didn't hear back from the agent, she started to worry.

After three weeks, Oz broke the decorum and wrote again to ask about "Dandelion." "He's my only child," she explained, "and, though I know it's already out of my hands, I do worry about his future. I want to make sure I've done my best by him."

It took the agent another week to write back. "Dandelion" had been introduced to nearly a dozen publishers, the agent reported, but unfortunately, he failed to make the right impression. It turned out, he didn't do well under pressure. He kept asking for mommy and other things he couldn't have. He didn't respond well to discipline. He refused to hold hands when walking down the street and darted into traffic with such force that the leash failed to hold him back. He was still alive, but just barely.

In short, no bids were forthcoming. The agent didn't see any point in trying again later. A basic character flaw made the child unacceptable to all the major publishers. "Being in San Francisco," the agent wrote, "you will be tempted to publish with an independent press. I would strongly counsel against this. Publishing with a small press makes you look desperate and abstruse. If you want to make it in New York, you have to work harder."

The agent sent the child back. When he arrived, Oz barely recognized him. He looked like a dandelion whose seeds had all blown away. He smelled like a sewer; his loaded diaper had not been changed during transit, but merely encased in a second pair of pants instead.

Together, Oz and her husband washed the child to get rid of the smell. They'd hoped that once his hair was clean and dry, it would curl back up, but they were disappointed. The hair remained thin and straight.

Oz returned to writing short fiction, while her husband cared for the child. "Let's see if you still like being tickled," he said, and chased after the boy, who promptly climbed from the dining room chair onto the table, nearly turning both over as he jumped to the floor. A step ahead of his father, he ran to his old bedroom, where Oz had recently moved her desk, and went to hide in her drawer.

"Dandelion" originally appeared in *Luggage: The short listed stories from Eyelands 8th international short story contest.*

Freddy Krueger is Not Real:
The Dream of a Burn Survivor

by Dina Peone

In the early 90s my older brother kept a cardboard cutout of Freddy Krueger in the darkest corner of his bedroom. Twice my height, this nightmare demon towered over me with a realistic grin and gaping overcooked skin. I was horrified, and yet pulled in by that festering face, those knife-fingers drawn open like a geisha fan. Why did he seem so pleased with himself? Maybe the scariest part about him was that he wore his scars like a trophy.

Whenever I walked past my brother's open door at night and the lights were off, I knew not to look inside because even a peripheral glimpse would send me running down the stairs. I knew that the two-ply corrugated devil wouldn't come to life but just incubate in a mischievous pose, yet it seemed that if I stared long enough he would step out of the frame with glowing yellow eyes and chase me under the covers, where I felt safest.

One night in my mid-teens, I was under the covers in my sister's bedroom, deep asleep, while flames spread from a nearby candle. I woke coughing and saw that a wicker loveseat was engulfed before a thick curtain of smoke blinded me. I choked out a hoarse, punctuated grumble in order to rouse my sister. It sounded nothing like me; rather, it came from the belly of a beast. She was also a deep sleeper and I'm thankful that she woke immediately, because in attempting to speak through the smoke I had used the last of my lung capacity. Voiceless and blinded, we fumbled and flailed, skin slipping like chunks of cheese from our arms. I fainted and she escaped.

By the time my mother found me, I had burned almost sixty percent of my body to the third-degree. I burned to the bone in my right hand, which resulted in gangrene and amputations. My face was mostly disfigured. The first time I looked at myself nude in a full-length mirror, I said, "I look like a monster." To this day (thirteen years later), when some children encounter me in public, they shriek and hide behind their mothers' legs.

Before my disfigurement I had only ever heard of burn survivors in movies. Krueger was my first exposure in "A Nightmare on Elm Street" (1984). His burns are punishment: a product of revenge from the parents of children he has murdered. After Krueger is found not guilty of his crimes, he returns to the boiler room where he would take his victims to die. The outraged parents find him there and set the building on fire, killing him. None of this is evidenced through plot but offered as back story tucked inside a dialogue between parent and child. Before this scene, which occurs more than halfway through the film, the reasons for Krueger's evildoing is left to the imagination. It's easy for an audience member to associate his cruelty with his disfigurement.

Krueger is not the only burn survivor represented in films as a villain. In a recent study of 32 English-language films that were made between 1933 and 2017, the Phoenix Society found that 50% of characters whose scars were confirmed or could be assumed to be burns were good but became evil after their injury and 62% sought revenge. Just to name a few from my research: Two-Face from "Batman Forever" (1995); Peyton Westlake from "Darkman" (1990); and Cropsy from "The Burning" (1981). Krueger, however, is the most famous. He played a crucial role in both the shaping of my childhood perception of what it means to burn and in the drama that was—and still is—the task of growing into my second skin. Krueger taught me that a burn survivor is something to be feared and avoided as if one's life depended on it. Such stigma only intensifies the sense of isolation that follows the touching of flames.

During the first year of my recovery, I moved swiftly through crowded streets and preferred shadowy corners. This way, I could have some measure of control over the facial contortions that occurred in reaction to my appearance. Eventually my knowing that people feared me became a source of empowerment. Last week a new acquaintance waited until I mentioned my burns before saying, "I bet there are many people who make the most stupid and ridiculous comments about your scars." I responded, "Nobody would dare. They're too afraid of me."

The fearfulness of Krueger's homicidal tendencies was apparently not enough to move audiences; he also had to serve as the embodiment of fear itself. (I think we can all agree that burning is one of the worst imaginable deaths.) And yet his burns were still not enough, so Krueger's creators threw in knife-fingers for good measure. According to the 2010 documentary "Never Sleep Again: The Elm Street Legacy," Krueger's glove-weapon is supposed to evoke a primitive fear of animals with claws. Robert Englund, the original actor who played Krueger, considers the symbolic benefits of the addition: "The claw extends Freddy. It extends his evil, it extends his anger." Not all burn survivors are angry *thankyouverymuch* and the ones who are need no makeshift appendage to express their emotions. All they have to do is stand there and be seen. Being burned is scary enough.

There is seemingly no end to the way that Krueger's creators capitalized on costume ideas that reinforced his repulsiveness. Filmmaker Wes Craven explains how Krueger's red and green striped sweater came to him after he read an article about the physical difficulty in seeing the two colors side by side. "I literally made him into a sort of painful optical effect," says Craven, who is either ignorant of the fact that burn survivors don't need tacky sweaters to achieve a painful optical effect, or he's insensitive to our struggle for beauty and sustained face-to-face interactions.

If I seem bitter, it's because Krueger tells me I should be. Although Krueger's burns are supplemental to his heinous history, their presence seems to justify his haunting behavior in the film. One looks back on the first scene, wherein he fashions his glove-weapon, with the understanding that maybe Krueger wouldn't have taken his violence to the next level if he hadn't been incinerated. This subtext lends itself to the notion that burn survivors should be so full of rage that it's almost a natural response to transfer their suffering to others. I wonder: when strangers first judge my character, do they assume that pissing me off will lead to their disembowelment? Maybe not, but I'd guess that ever since the film hit box offices people have associated a history of burning with a future of wrath at least on a subconscious level.

How much ethical consideration is given to the crafting of a Hollywood villain? Krueger's makeup artist relied on a medical textbook in which actual bodies like mine appeared. It seems that horror-industry producers care more about the aesthetic success of a cliché and less about a cliché's rippling consequences on the collective psyche.

A burn survivor is always a creature in the making. The worse the burn, the more reconstructive surgeries are required for the regaining of function and cosmetic satisfaction. As an acute burn survivor navigates the public eye, they must think of their appearance as both in flux and irreparably hideous. If, when I first examined my scars, I saw myself as a monster, then that is due in part to the revulsion that "A Nightmare on Elm Street" suggests people should experience in response to burns. Look for yourself at the number of cases in which child burn survivors are taunted by bullies with Krueger's name. He branded so many children with a vision of loathing and the disgraceful vocabulary to describe it. It is no wonder why burn survivors were so offended after the film's release; a bad reputation is everlasting.

I won't pretend that Krueger was the first example to teach that fire and enemies should go together. One glance at history will remind us that burning is reserved for individuals whose actions undermine collective power and safety (e.g. Joan of Arc, victims of the Salem witch trials, and other heretics who were burned at the stake). It's not Krueger's fault that in the deep seat of our minds there forms the vivid picture of a mob carrying torches to the homes of unwanted anomalies. An adversarial stance toward the disfigured is practically an evolutionary response: we are biologically programmed, for the survival of our species, to gravitate toward the beautiful and to banish the ugly. As long as there have been stories, the beautiful has been paired with the good and ugly with evil. Even if the film and its sequels could be magically erased, the psychological foundations for the creation of an icon like Krueger would remain firmly in place. My complaints are ash in the wind. It feels good to scatter them.

As I got older I felt increasingly silly for running past my brother's door, so I would pause for a moment and test the cardboard fiend daringly. If my eyes didn't play tricks on me—casting a shimmer along his stainless steel knuckles—I would grow brave and inch into the dark. I would make it right up to the fibers in his red and green striped sweater, reach my trembling fingers around his flat waist, and pull back and forth to ensure he was fake. Once, the display tipped over on me and I fled screaming. Right now I'd gladly go back and let that two-dimensional fool lie on me. *Oh Freddy*, I'd say. *I know you're not real. You weigh practically nothing.*

Contributors

Margaret Adams's stories and essays have appeared in *Joyland Magazine*, *The Pinch Journal*, *Monkeybicycle*, and *The Threepenny Review*, among other publications. She won the *Blue Mesa Review* 2018 Nonfiction Contest, the *Pacifica Literary Review* 2017 Fiction Contest, and was a *Best American Essays 2019* Notable. She is an associate fiction editor for *JMWW*. She currently lives on the AZ/NM border in the Navajo Nation where she works as a nurse practitioner.

Threa Almontaser is a Yemeni-American writer, translator, and multimedia artist from New York City. She received her MFA from North Carolina State University and is the recipient of fellowships from *Tin House*, Community of Writers, the Fine Arts Work Center, and the Kerouac House. She is the winner of Alternating Current's Unsilenced Grant for Muslim American Women Writers and *Tinderbox Poetry Journal's* Brett Elizabeth Jenkins Poetry Prize, among other honors. Nominated or included in the Pushcart Prize, Best New Poets, and Best of the Net, her work has previously appeared or is forthcoming from Random House, *The Offing*, *American Literary Review*, *The Adroit Journal*, *Wildness*, and elsewhere.

Derek Annis is the author of *Neighborhood of Gray Houses*, which will be released by Lost Horse Press in 2020. Derek lives in Spokane, Washington, and holds an MFA from Eastern Washington University. Their poems have appeared in *The Account, Colorado Review, Epiphany, The Gettysburg Review, The Missouri Review Online,* and other journals.

Katherine Ayars has been published in multiple literary magazines and has twice been nominated for a Pushcart Prize. She has an undergraduate degree from NYU in drama and psychology. She holds two MFAs in Creative Writing (Simmons and Boston University) and has taught at Boston University for three years. She is also a SAG actor and a visual artist—body painting, canvas painting, neon, and photography. She was awarded the Pinsky Fellowship in Fiction, which afforded her the opportunity to live and write in Thailand and Bhutan for three months.

Recipient of the Edna St. Vincent Millay and Red Wheelbarrow Poetry Prizes, Partridge Boswell is the author of *Some Far Country* (Grolier Poetry Prize). His poems have recently surfaced in *The Gettysburg Review, Salmagundi, The American Poetry Review, Poetry Ireland Review, Plume,* and elsewhere. Co-founder of Bookstock literary festival and the poetry/music group Los Lorcas, he teaches at Burlington Writers Workshop and lives with his family in Vermont.

Tom Boswell is a writer, photographer and community organizer living in Madison, Wisconsin. His poetry has appeared in *Atlanta Review*, *Rattle*, *Poet Lore*, *Potomac Review*, *Two Thirds North*, and other journals, as well as the anthology *New Poetry from the Midwest 2017*. He has won national competitions judged by Tony Hoagland, Luis Alberto Urrea, and Robert Cording. His chapbook *Midwestern Heart* won the Codhill Poetry Chapbook Award. A second chapbook, *Neighbors*, was published by Evening Street Press and won the Helen Kay Chapbook Prize.

George Choundas is a former FBI agent with fiction and nonfiction in over fifty publications, including *The Best Small Fictions 2015*. He is a winner of the New Millennium Award for Fiction and a two-time Pushcart Prize nominee. His short story collection, *The Making Sense of Things*, was awarded the Ronald Sukenick Innovative Fiction Prize as well as shortlisted for the Katherine Anne Porter Prize in Short Fiction, the Robert C. Jones Prize for Short Prose, and the St. Lawrence Book Award for Fiction.

Karlyn Coleman is an award-winning writer, teacher, and creative collaborator based in Minneapolis. Her short stories and essays have appeared in *McSweeney's Internet Tendency*, *Water-Stone Review*, *Paper Darts*, *Revolver*, and *Crab Orchard Review*. Her honors include a Sustainable Arts Grant, a Minnesota Emerging Writers Grant, and a Loft Literary Center Mentor Series award. She also writes under the pen name K.R. Coleman. Recently she has started a walking book club where literary discussions take place while strolling around the many lakes in her city.

Rebecca Foust's most recent book is *Paradise Drive*. Recognitions include the James Hearst Poetry Prize, the American Literary Review Fiction Prize, the Constance Rooke Creative Nonfiction Award, fellowships from MacDowell and Sewanee, and recent appointment as poet laureate of Marin County. Foust is the poetry editor and writes a weekly column for *Women's Voices for Change*, and is an assistant editor reading fiction for *Narrative Magazine*.

Sean Gill is a writer and filmmaker who won the 2016 *Sonora Review* Fiction Prize, the 2017 *River Styx* Micro-Fiction Contest, and *The Cincinnati Review's* 2018 Robert and Adele Schiff Award in Prose. He has studied with Werner Herzog and Juan Luis Buñuel, documented public defenders for *National Geographic*, and was an artist-in-residence at the Bowery Poetry Club from 2011-2012. Other recent work has been published or is forthcoming in *The Iowa Review*, *McSweeney's*, *Carolina Quarterly*, and *ZYZZYVA*.

Carlos Andrés Gómez is a graduate of the MFA Program for Writers at Warren Wilson College. Winner of the 2015 Lucille Clifton Poetry Prize and a three-time Pushcart Prize nominee, his work has appeared in the *New England Review*, *Beloit Poetry Journal*, *The Rumpus*, *Rattle*, *Chorus: A Literary Mixtape* (Simon & Schuster, 2012), and elsewhere.

torrin a. greathouse is a transgender cripple-punk & MFA candidate at the University of Minnesota. She is the author of *boy/girl/ghost* (TAR Chapbook Series, 2018) & assistant editor of *The Shallow Ends*. Their work is published in *Poetry*, *The New York Times*, *The Kenyon Review*, and elsewhere. She is the youngest ever winner of the Poetry Foundation's J. Howard and Barbara M.J. Wood Prize.

Stephanie Hutton is a writer and Clinical Psychologist in the UK. She was shortlisted for the Bridport Prize, the Bristol Short Story Prize, and the Bath Novella-in-Flash Award. Her novella *Three Sisters of Stone* is published with Ellipsis Zine. She can be found at stephaniehutton.com.

Ingrid Jendrzejewski grew up in Vincennes, Indiana, studied creative writing at the University of Evansville, then physics at the University of Cambridge. She has been published in places like *Passages North*, *The Los Angeles Review*, *The Conium Review*, *Jellyfish Review*, and *Rattle*, and is editor-in-chief at *FlashBack Fiction* and a flash fiction editor at *JMWW*. When not writing, she enjoys cryptic crosswords, puzzle hunts, and the game of go. Links to Ingrid's work can be found at ingridj.com. She tweets @LunchOn-Tuesday.

Zoë Johnson is a queer transgender non-binary writer living in Lansing, Michigan. They are an enrolled member of the Sault Ste. Marie Tribe of Chippewa Indians, and a current graduate student in the creative writing MFA program at the Institute of American Indian Arts. Their writing was shortlisted for *PRISM International*'s 2019 Jacob Zilber Prize for Short Fiction, and has been published by *PULP Literature*, *Sonora Review Online*, and *Plentitude Magazine*. Work of theirs is forthcoming in the 2019 ENOUGH Anthology from *Public Poetry*, and in the second edition of *Trans Bodies, Trans Selves* from Oxford University Press.

Miriam Karmel's stories have appeared in *Bellevue Literary Review*, *Water~Stone Review*, *Coe Review*, *Bacopa Review*, *Alaska Quarterly Review*, and elsewhere. She is the recipient of the Moment Karma Fiction Award, the First Fiction contest sponsored by Holy Cow! Press, and others. Her debut novel, *Being Esther*, was published in 2013. *Subtle Variations and Other Stories* appeared in 2017.

Joy Kennedy-O'Neill's stories have been published in *Nature: Futures*, *Galaxy's Edge*, *The Cimarron Review*, *Daily Science Fiction*, and *Strange Horizons*, among others. Her story "Heron Girl" was the winner of the 2018 Gris-Gris Flash Fiction Contest. She teaches English for a small college on the Texas Gulf Coast. She can be found at joykennedyoneill.com.

Margaret Koger is an educator in Boise, Idaho. Her poems appear in numerous publications, including *Amsterdam Quarterly*, *Red Rock Review*, *Collective Unrest*, *Headway*, and *Voice of Eve*. Her poem "Ripe Figs" was a finalist in the

2018 Joy Bale Boone Poetry Prize at *The Heartland Review* and "The Bears of Redfish Lake" won the 2019 summer poetry competition at Forbidden Peak Press.

Suki Litchfield is an award-winning writer whose fiction has appeared in a number of literary journals, including *Down in the Dirt, Toasted Cheese,* and *Mudrock: Stories and Tales.* She lives in Florida.

Isabel Mae is a poet and criminal justice reform activist from Ann Arbor, Michigan. She received the 2017 Avery Hopwood and Jule Hopwood Award for Undergraduate Poetry from the University of Michigan. Her poetry also appears in *Bone Bouquet Issue 8.2.* She currently teaches English in Granada, Spain.

Lauren Lynn Matheny is a writer of fiction and nonfiction. She received her MFA in fiction from Colorado State University in 2018. Her work has won prizes from *Third Coast Magazine* and *Literal Latte.*

Steve McDonald's second full-length book, *Credo,* was a finalist in the 2016 Brick Road Poetry Press competition. His chapbook *Golden Fish / Dark Pond* won the 2014 Comstock Review Chapbook contest. Individual poems have won awards from *Tiferet, Nimrod, Beyond Baroque, Passager, Sow's Ear,* and others, including *Best New Poets 2010,* and have appeared in *Boulevard, The Atlanta Review, Rattle, The Crab Creek Review, Paterson Literary Review,* and elsewhere. He is Professor Emeritus of English and retired Dean of Languages and Literature at Palomar College in San Marcos, California.

Karen McIntyre's work has appeared in *A Clean, Well-Lighted Place for Literature* and *The Lascaux Prize 2015*. She lives in New York City with her husband and daughter.

Bailey Merlin holds an MFA in fiction from Butler University. Her work has been published or is forthcoming in *Crack the Spine*, *Not Your Mother's Breast Milk*, *The Indianapolis Review*, among others. She lives and writes in Boston. Find more of her work at baileymerlin.com.

Robert Murray earned an MFA from Vermont College of Fine Arts. His memoir *A Chicken Hawk Comes Home* was published by North of Eden Press. A longtime singer-songwriter, he has released four albums of contemporary acoustic music.

Dina Peone is a native of Saugerties, New York and a graduate of the University of Iowa's Nonfiction Writing Program, where she taught the university's first online course in nonfiction. She is presently a visiting lecturer at the University of Chicago. Dina's work has appeared in *The Sarah Lawrence Review*, *Poor Yorick*, *Chronogram*, *Come to Woodstock*, *Slate*, and elsewhere. She is at work on a memoir about escaping a house fire with severe burns when she was a morbid, self-destructive teenager.

Michelle Ross is the author of *There's So Much They Haven't Told You*, which won the 2016 Moon City Press Short Fiction Award. Her fiction has recently appeared or is forthcoming in *Alaska Quarterly Review*, *Colorado Review*, *Nashville Review*, *Electric Literature's* Recommended Reading, *TriQuarterly*, and other venues. She is fiction editor of *Atticus Review*.

Claire Scott is an award winning poet who has received multiple Pushcart Prize nominations. Her work has been accepted by *Atlanta Review*, *Bellevue Literary Review*, *New Ohio Review*, *Enizagam*, and *Healing Muse*, among others. Claire is the author of *Waiting to be Called* and a co-author of *Unfolding in Light: A Sisters' Journey in Photography and Poetry*.

Leona Sevick's work appears in *The Journal*, *Crab Orchard Review*, *The Normal School*, and other journals. Her work also appears in *The Golden Shovel Anthology: New Poems Honoring Gwendolyn Brooks*. She is the 2017 Press 53 Poetry Award Winner for *Lion Brothers*, her first full-length collection. She can be reached at leonasevick.com.

A member of the Colorado Poets Center, Amie Sharp's work has appeared in numerous literary journals including *Atticus Review*, *Badlands*, *Bellevue Literary Review*, *BlazeVOX*, and *Burningword Literary Journal*. She has performed at the Bridgewater International Poetry Festival and the Houston Poetry Fest, and she spent the summer of 2018 as artist-in-residence at the Sabina Cultural Association in Casaprota, Italy.

Sue Showalter is an aspiring poet and fiction writer. She resides in Austin, Texas with her musician husband. "Review" is her first publication.

Julie Marie Wade is the author of ten collections of poetry and prose, including the recently released *Same-Sexy Marriage: A Novella in Poems* and *The Unrhymables: Collaborations in Prose*, co-authored with Denise Duhamel. She is an Associate Professor of Creative Writing at Florida International University in Miami.

Clare Weze won a Northern Writers' Award for her forthcoming short-story collection. Her work has been shortlisted in several literary prizes, including Bridport 2018. Her short fiction can be found in anthologies by Aesthetica, Bridge House Publishing, Curiosity Quills, the Bath Flash Fiction Award and Wonderbox Publishing. Her writing has also appeared online in *The Conglomerate* and *Reflex Fiction*, and accompanies the CD of "Clinch Mountain" by musician Fionn Kay-Lavelle. She is represented by The Good Literary Agency.

Mary Wolff studied creative writing at the University of South Florida. She currently lives and writes in Orlando.

Her work appears in *The Write Room*, *Black Heart Magazine*, and *34th Parallel Magazine*.

Olga Zilberbourg's English-language debut, *Like Water and Other Stories*, was published in 2019 by WTAW Press. She grew up in St. Petersburg, Russia and makes her home in San Francisco. Her fiction has appeared in *Alaska Quarterly Review*, *Feminist Studies*, *World Literature Today*, *Tin House*'s The Open Bar, and *Narrative Magazine*, among others. She serves as a co-facilitator of the San Francisco Writers Workshop.

Made in USA - North Chelmsford, MA
1062749_9780985166694
03.25.2020 1154